There's No Such Thing as Public Speaking

Make Any Presentation or Speech as Persuasive as a One-on-One Conversation

Jeanette and Roy Henderson

Prentice Hall Press

A PRENTICE HALL BOOK
Published by the Penguin Group
Penguin Group (USA) Inc.
375 Hudson Street, New York, New York 10014, USA
Penguin Group (Canada), 90 Eglinton Avenue East, Suite 700, Toronto, Ontario M4P 2Y3, Canada
(a division of Pearson Penguin Canada Inc.)
Penguin Books Ltd., 80 Strand, London WC2R 0RL, England
Penguin Group Ireland, 25 St. Stephen's Green, Dublin 2, Ireland
(a division of Penguin Books Ltd.)
Penguin Group (Australia), 250 Camberwell Road, Camberwell, Victoria 3124, Australia
(a division of Pearson Australia Group Pty. Ltd.)
Penguin Books India Pvt. Ltd., 11 Community Centre, Panchsheel Park, New Delhi—110 017, India
Penguin Group (NZ), Cnr. Airborne and Rosedale Roads, Albany, Auckland 1310, New Zealand
(a division of Pearson New Zealand Ltd.)
Penguin Books (South Africa) (Pty.) Ltd., 24 Sturdee Avenue, Rosebank, Johannesburg 2196,
South Africa

Penguin Books Ltd., Registered Offices: 80 Strand, London WC2R 0RL, England

While the authors have made every effort to provide accurate telephone numbers and Internet addresses at the time of publication, neither the publisher nor the authors assume any responsibility for errors, or for changes that occur after publication. Further, the publisher does not have any control over and does not assume any responsibility for author or third-party websites or their content.

THERE'S NO SUCH THING AS PUBLIC SPEAKING

First edition: January 2007

Prentice Hall trade paperback ISBN: 978-0-7352-0415-7

An application to register this book for cataloging has been submitted to the Library of Congress.

PRINTED IN THE UNITED STATES OF AMERICA

10   9   8   7

Most Prentice Hall books are available at special quantity discounts for bulk purchases for sales promotions, premiums, fund-raising, or educational use. Special books, or book excerpts, can also be created to fit specific needs. For details, write: Special Markets, The Berkley Publishing Group, 375 Hudson Street, New York, New York 10014.

Praise for the Coaching Techniques of Jeanette and Roy Henderson

"Thank you for working with me at our recent National Convention. This is not the first time you have helped me make a speech better than it would have been otherwise."

—William H. Frist, MD,
Majority Leader, United States Senate

"Without exception, the staff is of the opinion that Roy and Jeanette Henderson are far and away the finest public-speaking instructors we have been exposed to."

—Mark R. Knowles, Executive Director,
National Pharmaceutical Council

"This year's meetings were spectacular, organized, and very professional. The meetings were virtually flawless, truly a compliment to your professionalism."

—Ed Hermes, Director,
Corporate Year-End Meetings,
Procter & Gamble

"I'm pleased to say my talk received rave reviews. But even more amazing to me was the metamorphosis I saw among office workers who had never addressed an audience. From the first rehearsal to the final performance, the change was incredible: from a shy, scared person who didn't want to do it in the first place, to the confident, dynamic presenter who played to loud applause and probably would have taken the show on the road if she had the opportunity. It was a great experience, and I thank you for your guidance."

—Don R. Lee, Vice President,
Norwich Eaton Pharmaceuticals, Inc.

CONTENTS

CONTENTS

Preface

The only books that influence us are those for which we are ready, and which have gone a little farther down our particular path than we have yet got ourselves.
—TWO CHEERS FOR DEMOCRACY (1951)

People talk. It's natural, part of being human. We all have one-on-one conversations every day without giving them a second thought. Then one day, someone asks you to speak to a group, and something happens. Suddenly, everything you ever knew about speaking seems foreign, strange, unfathomable. You don't even know where to start, much less how to finish. What to say, how to say it, what to do, how to do it. It all seems impossibly difficult and unreasonably frightening. What do you do?

We first became aware of this interesting mystery when ordinary people like lawyers and salespeople began attending our acting workshops. As lifelong members of the entertainment industry as performers, directors, producers, and staging experts, we understood the need for actors to hone their skills, but for lawyers and executives? Why did anyone need help just to talk like themselves? We became intrigued.

We decided to turn our attention to the subject of public speaking, persuasion, communication, and the entire industry it includes. We started out doing what most people do when they want to learn something new, and just what you are doing right now by opening this book: We looked for knowledge wherever we could.

We studied everything we could get our hands on. We read textbooks, business books, and pop culture books; watched videotapes; went to seminars, workshops, and classes. We did everything we could to try to understand how others taught this apparently complicated subject, though it didn't seem all that complicated to us. We continued to push forward, thinking we were missing something, seeking the light at the end of the tunnel.

Finally, we had our epiphany. After years of effort and study, we eventually realized that just about everything we had read or heard or seen of everyone else teaching the subject was, in a word, gobbledygook. Old wives' tales mixed with unsubstantiated claims, a disorganized collection of unscientific approaches, anecdotal stories that could never be applied to other situations, and in many cases, just plain absurd notions that were passed from one generation to the next without thought or question (Imagine your audience naked? Where in the world does that get you?). It was time to start over.

So that's what we did. We changed our strategy and went straight to the horse's mouth. We watched films and videos of countless speeches, listened to old-time radio broadcasts, read transcripts of all of the great (and not so great) speeches that we could get, and added the information we gleaned to our already decades-long understanding of the performance industry. We started our analysis from scratch, with the idea that we needed to distill down everything we found to the most fundamental, basic elements possible, so they could then be applied to *any* communication situation, whether it was a conversation between individuals or a speech before thousands.

Then we put it in order, so that we could train people in a step-by-step process, building personal knowledge in a sensible, logical, and practical way, unlike anything we had been able to find in our own quest for understanding what makes the perfect presentation.

Our philosophy is simple: "There's no such thing as public speaking." Consider the speeches that were made by President Ronald Reagan. Yes, they were speeches, yet they never felt like speeches. It felt like he was in our living room having a private conversation with us. That is the goal of the perfect presentation: to realize that the number of people listening is irrelevant; you are simply having a one-on-one conversation with a lot of people at once.

When we began using our system to train lawyers, executives, politicians, and many extremely experienced speakers, we were amazed at how many would make the comment, "I've been speaking for years, yet I've never heard this advice before. It makes so much sense, why didn't someone tell me this twenty years ago?" We knew we were on the right track.

We grew a long client list of corporations, businesses, and politicians, and our methods have changed the lives and livelihoods of many people. Yet we continued to watch an overall decline in speaking skills in this country, and realized that we had to reach further to stop that decline.

That is the simple purpose of this book. Whereas many "experts" tend to complicate the simple, the goal of this book is to simplify the complicated. It is filled with techniques, methods, and eureka moments that you will be able to use immediately and will remember for the rest of your life. We promise that after you've read this book, you will never be able to give (or watch) a presentation in the same way again.

Now our goal is for you to take the knowledge within these pages and apply it in what you do, and what you see others do. Whether you are speaking to your local service club, your peers in a business meeting, or to your nation, this book will provide you the tools and skills you need so that you will know what you are doing every step of the way.

Only by having more skilled presenters and more discerning listeners will we ever be able to reverse the sad trend of deteriorating communication skills that have become the norm in recent decades. By becoming better speakers, and demanding others do the same, we can all breathe life back into this dying yet immensely important skill—and convey our messages, great and small, with the immediacy and impact they (and all audiences) deserve.

There's
No Such Thing as
Public Speaking

PART 1

The Six Truths
of Human Interaction

It's Alive, It's Alive!

For every action, there is an equal and opposite reaction.
—NEWTON'S THIRD LAW OF MOTION

Every time a tennis ball hits a racket, a rocket escapes the grip of earth's gravity, or the stroke of an oar propels water in one direction and its boat in another, the existence of Isaac Newton's indisputable, fundamental principle of physics is clearly demonstrated in all its undeniable glory. It is undoubtedly the most clearly understood and widely accepted principle in all of the physical sciences.

Somewhat less obviously, it is also a principle that pervades and contributes toward every human interaction: Whenever we give, we expect someone to take; whenever we teach, we expect someone to learn; and whenever we speak, we expect someone to listen.

Because of this Cause and Effect relationship, we must never view a listener as passive or uninvolved just because they are "simply" listening. The listener is active. The listener is responsive. The listener will react to whatever stimuli we choose to use. The listener is alive!

We see obvious examples of this kind of human interaction every day, even before someone becomes our listener. When you deliberately make eye contact with a clerk at a store with whom you want to speak, you've taken an action to which you expect a reaction: for that person to come and help you. When you look down at the elevator floor, you are taking an action to which you expect a reaction: that others on the elevator will be discouraged from interacting with you.

These are simple examples of how Newton's Third Law of Cause and Effect controls all human interaction; one person does something, instigating a Cause, which subsequently creates a certain Effect in another person. All this before even a word is spoken!

Every time two people come together, a Cause and Effect relationship immediately and invariably begins. One person will put in certain actions, and the other person will react to them. In an ideal one-on-one conversation, the give and take will be well-balanced between the two, with both putting in equal actions and both providing equal reactions.

In the case of making a presentation to more than one person, however, there is an inevitable imbalance, because one person will do most of the talking, and the others will do most of the listening. The person doing most of the talking, therefore, becomes "the Presenter" (who, for convenience, is referred to as "he" throughout this book). The person who is doing most of the listening will henceforth be called "the Reactor" (and is referred to as "she" throughout the book).

In every human interaction, **the Presenter puts in the Causes, and the response of the Reactor is the Effect.**

4

Therefore, as the Presenter, you must clearly understand that everything you do, every move you make will have a consequence, and the Reactor will respond accordingly. When you wish those consequences to be of a certain nature, you must put in the correct actions, or Causes, to get the appropriate reactions, or Effects, you desire.

So when you want to earn the support of someone to win a job, persuade voters, make a sale, or have any definite result from your conversation, you must put in the right Causes in order to provoke the desired Effect from your Reactor.

By the same token, should a Reactor fall asleep during your conversation, that is a "reaction" provoked by your actions as well. That means you can never use the excuse that you had a "bad" audience, as they were only reacting to the actions *you* put in.

Provoking a response from your Reactor is your responsibility as the Presenter. The Reactor is merely compelled by Newton's Third Law to respond to your actions. Knowing the incontrovertible reality of this law gives you, the Presenter, a powerful tool that you must now use, fully and carefully.

The first obligation of this newly understood responsibility is to make sure that you know what Effect you wish to instigate before you speak. As obvious as this sounds, it's a safe bet that you, like the rest of us, have had to sit through presentations where, in the end, you had no idea what the Presenter's point or purpose was, and were left wondering why he (and you) wasted your time.

Once you have determined the overall result you want, you can now go about the business of figuring out what Causes you need to put in to get that Effect. Simply determining what specific end goal you want to accomplish as a result of your conversation will put you miles ahead of the pack!

TRUTH #1, then, is simply to realize that every listener is a Reactor, bound to respond to the Causes you put in, and that you must know what Effect or reaction you want before you ever speak.

If You Try, Sometimes You Get What You Need

I can't get no . . . satisfaction.
—THE ROLLING STONES

I just need enough to tide me over until I need more.
—BILL HOEST

The most constant, fundamental drive we humans experience through-out our lives is the ongoing struggle for the satisfaction of our needs. It is the unforgiving, undeniable derivative of our innate animal instinct for survival.

In essence, the only answer to the simplest and most fundamental philosophical question, "Why are we here?" is the equally simple and fundamental answer, "To have our needs satisfied."

Our lives are driven by a ceaseless effort to satisfy our needs. Every moment of every day we are consumed with the attempt to satisfy many needs: food, drink, housing, companionship, comfort, security, approval, greater compensation, happiness, and whatever else appeals to us at any given moment.

We are constantly taking action to satisfy these needs, putting in the Causes to create the Effect of having our needs satisfied. As soon as one need is filled, we're on to another need, and we begin to seek out ways to satisfy *that* need and the next, and the next.

Most of the time, we are quite capable of satisfying many of our needs on our own and proceed to do so without a second thought. When we are hungry, a quick, solo trip to the refrigerator satisfies that need. Yet back in our early caveman days, satisfying our hunger was much more complicated and often required the help of others in order to accomplish it.

Imagine this scenario: You're hungry, you need food, but that mammoth you've noticed outside your cave is too big and runs too fast. You realize that you must get someone's help in order to be able to slay the mammoth. The quickest way to get that help is to use your newly discovered ability to talk. You recognize you must begin a conversation that will put in the Causes that will have the desired Effect: getting help to slay the mammoth.

In fact, the reason communication developed in the first place was because it was the fastest way to get others to help us satisfy all of the needs we couldn't satisfy on our own. To this day, it's still the main reason we ever start a conversation in the first place.

So, first and foremost, before you begin a conversation of any kind, you must know what need you intend to have satisfied as a result, what Effect you desire. Once that need has been identified ("I want mammoth steak," or "I want love and affection," or "I want to be president of the United States"), then and only then will you be able to begin to put in the Causes to achieve the desired Effect.

Therefore, **TRUTH #2** requires that you determine what needs you wish to have satisfied as a result of your conversation. From there, you can begin to put in the Causes to achieve the result of having that need satisfied.

What's Good for the One Is Good for the Many

Norm . . .
—CAST OF THE TV SERIES *CHEERS*

By far, the strongest form of communication possible is a one-on-one conversation. No other form of communication can share more experiences, reach greater heights of awareness, promote a higher level of understanding, or inspire more new ideas than two people deeply involved in a single, face-to-face exchange.

This should be expected, as this is the first kind of communication that we learned both as a species and as individuals. From the moment we first hear our parents' voices as they nurture us, we human beings observe and participate in countless one-on-one conversations. Over time, we store enough examples from these everyday experiences to develop a vast memory bank of knowledge about how humans communicate.

We learn what types of physical behaviors go with what types of verbal communications. We understand what mannerisms to pay attention to, how a person's voice varies between love and discipline even when the words are the same, how body language telegraphs intent, and thousands of other subtle aspects of human interaction.

This huge memory bank is the registry of *norms*, a personal database, if you will, of all of our acceptable communications behaviors. Because we have more experience with one-on-one conversations than with any other type of communication, this registry of norms is primarily based on those experiences.

In fact, these norms provide us with the tools necessary to determine a great deal about the accuracy and believability of any human interaction. Whenever we observe or participate in any conversation, we unconsciously compare it to what we already "know" from our vast memory bank to be "correct," and make judgments accordingly.

Whenever someone fails to meet our norms of behavior, by exhibiting actions that are inconsistent with what our memory bank indicates they should be under the circumstances, internal alarm bells go off. Whenever these alarm bells are ringing, we find ourselves distracted from what the person is saying, because we're trying to figure out what's wrong.

These incongruities between someone's actions and our unconscious norms often register quite subtly—so subtly, in fact, that many people refer to the discovery of these hidden discrepancies as "intuition." While we are often unable to put our finger on exactly why we find a particular person or conversation difficult to believe or trust, we still just *know* that *something* is wrong, and can only explain that uneasiness by attributing it to our own indefinable sense of intuition. In reality, we're feeling this sense of uneasiness because the other person's behavior conflicts with our memory bank of norms.

In a typical everyday conversation, we both observe and perform these norms of communication without giving them a second thought. Our actions, regardless of whether we are the Presenter or the Reactor, will appear perfectly normal as long as we aren't thinking about them. When the situation changes, however, such as when we find ourselves speaking in front of a group of people, or perhaps being confronted by one very important person, we sense that somehow our behavior should change, too.

Suddenly, we start to think more carefully about what we're doing and what we're saying. We recognize that it's no longer a normal one-on-one conversation; it's something more. We feel we must somehow change what we would normally do to accommodate that difference, though we may have no idea how or why.

The more we consciously think about what to say and do, the farther we stray from our norms. The farther we stray from our norms, the more likely we are to set off those alarm bells. When alarm bells are ringing, the Reactor will respond only to those alarm bells, not to anything else a Presenter might be doing or saying.

It should be apparent, then, that your first and foremost need as a Presenter is to make sure that your communication style does not set off any alarm bells in your Reactor (your audience). You must be sure that you meet the *norms of one-on-one behavior*, regardless of the venue, to ensure your message will be believed and trusted.

Logically, then, the best approach is to first understand exactly what happens when we speak to just one person in a normal conversation. Once you take the time to identify what is considered the norm and why, you can then learn how to replicate that norm in any venue, in front of any size audience.

This is the essence of outstanding presenting and speaking—to understand each and every element of the norms of a one-on-one conversation. Once you know what happens normally, you will then be able to replicate them in a way that captures the strength of that one-on-one conversation no matter how many other people are listening!

TRUTH #3, then, is simply to understand that *every communication is just a conversation, no matter how many people may be listening*. Everything you say and do at the podium must meet the one-on-one norms of your audience, regardless of the number of Re-actors. What's good for talking to the *one* is good for talking to the *many*.

First Contact

There is neither East nor West, Border, nor Breed, nor Birth,
When two strong men stand face to face, tho' they come from
the ends of earth!
—RUDYARD KIPLING

The first door to open in every communication is that of **Acknowledgment**.

Every creature on earth has instinctively devised some method of acknowledging the presence of another, either of its own or some other species. An acknowledgment provides each the opportunity to determine the nature and intent of the other, whether it be friend or foe, or worthy of notice, avoidance, or confrontation. Like dogs sizing each other up, they must sniff winds, faces, and other sundry places before deciding what kind of relationship exists between them at that first moment, and what might potentially develop.

The same is true for human beings. It is necessary for us to acknowledge others nearby, to determine whether to flee or fight, to talk or remain silent, to open or close the door to further conversation.

Acknowledgment is the first essential and mandatory need, for both the Presenter and the Reactor, which must be satisfied prior to the advancement of any personal contact.

Acknowledgment in humans always begins the same way; it requires that both parties turn their entire bodies to face one another, shoulders squared up, looking at each other straight in the eye. This is known as a *full frontal stance*. Regardless of culture, the full frontal stance is the universally understood way that humans initially acknowledge one another.

Consider what happens when a full frontal stance and eye contact is ignored. When we look at the floor in an elevator, or when a clerk turns away from us as we stand at a counter in a store, we recognize that any potential conversation is stopped dead in its tracks, simply because there is no full frontal stance, therefore no acknowledgment.

As simplistic as this may seem, a full frontal stance and direct eye contact are necessary to achieve acknowledgment, and acknowledgment is necessary to allow a conversation to move forward. So when a conversation is desired, it must always begin with an Acknowledgment.

As Presenter, simply turn to your intended Reactor with a full frontal stance and direct eye contact. The Reactor will almost automatically turn to you with a corresponding full frontal stance and eye contact, as that is her instinctive norm. Congratulations, you have just put in the first intentional Cause and have been rewarded with the first deliberate Effect. You've opened the first door toward further conversation.

We've just described what happens almost without thinking in every one-on-one conversation. When the venue or situation changes, this need to be acknowledged must still be satisfied, in *every* venue.

How to make proper Acknowledgment in alternative venues will be discussed in detail in later chapters. For now, simply be aware that **TRUTH #4** is that *Acknowledgment is the first step in creating the opportunity to start a conversation.*

To Shake or Not to Shake

Give a man a free hand and he'll try to put it all over you.
—MAE WEST IN *KLONDIKE ANNIE* (1936)

Come gather 'round people, wherever you roam . . .
—BOB DYLAN

Once the need for Acknowledgment has been satisfied with a full frontal stance and direct eye contact, it will immediately be replaced by the next essential need: that of **Acceptance**.

Ever since human beings first walked on this earth, we have experienced the overwhelming need to gather together. We learned very early in our human history that failure to be included in some kind of group generally threatened our existence. Failure to at least attract a mate (the most critical one-on-one conversation of all!) spelled extinction.

It was much safer and more secure to be part of a multitude, because it increased our odds for survival and for finding a suitable mate. Clearly, excommunication from a group (a most appropriate term, when you think about it) almost assuredly meant a shortened life span for those unfortunate enough to be expelled.

Therefore, in order to insure our survival, we were compelled to gather in groups. The more successful the group, the larger it became. Families became clans, clans became tribes, tribes became nations. These successful groups became the ones others desired to join, as it improved our chances of survival. Acceptance within a group became an essential need.

Once a group was established, it became necessary to be able to identify members of that group from potentially dangerous nonmembers. Therefore, each group established a cultural norm of acceptance. Handshakes (secret or otherwise), bowing (with or without gestures), and kissing cheeks (one cheek or two) are all examples of how human cultures have developed a means of identifying members of their own culture.

It should be no surprise that all of these gestures of Acceptance begin from a full frontal stance. That's because the moment the need for Acknowledgment is satisfied with a universally recognized full frontal stance, it is immediately replaced with the need for a culturally specific gesture of Acceptance. When that Acceptance is then offered in the way we expect, such as with a handshake in the Western culture, the progression of the conversation will continue uninterrupted, with barely a moment's notice.

We understand that the moment we recognize that the Acceptance being offered meets our norm, chances are the rest of the norms of conversation will be met as well. This makes it easier for us to trust that conversation, simply because we know that should our norms be violated, we will immediately recognize it, and will know to become suspicious. We trust our "intuition," our memory bank of norms, to tell us so.

In cases when an alternative Acceptance is unexpectedly offered, such as a bow or an approach to the cheek for a kiss or a hug, there will be a moment of hesitation, a moment when the Reactor must consider whether to allow herself to be accepted into foreign territory, as it were. Alarm bells begin to sound, signaling a warning she cannot ignore.

This happens because any movement outside of our cultural norm is, for a moment, the same as if the Presenter were to put up his fists in a boxer's stance. The Reactor's imbedded instincts are to protect herself from anything outside her norm; therefore, her intuitive alarm bells will go off when any incongruity occurs. She must then check herself and reason whether the action was a threat or a simple faux pas by the Presenter.

One thing the Reactor knows for sure is that the Presenter has demonstrated different cultural norms, which will require her to be more cautious during her conversation, lest a cultural misunderstanding of those alternative norms occur, causing mistrust when none was intended, or worse, creating trust when no trust was intended.

In cases when we know that the Presenter is a member of our group, that he, in fact, shares our cultural norms in every predictable way, alarm bells can still be set off when he ignores those cultural norms. Let's say that he has, indeed, turned to you in a full frontal stance in Acknowledgment. Suppose you reach out your hand to his to be shaken, and it is ignored.

For a moment, you will be confused, even insulted, because the Acceptance you had expected, had needed at that moment, didn't occur.

19

Further conversation would be very strained, simply because this basic action of Acceptance was ignored, and the natural reaction would be to feel uncomfortable because of it. Whether that discomfort was intentional or not doesn't matter; the result is the same: The alarm bells are ringing.

Now reverse that. Suppose the Presenter skipped the full frontal Acknowledgment entirely. From a profile position, he just reached out across his body to shake your hand without turning to you. Wouldn't that seem awkward and unwelcoming to you?

That's because offering Acceptance by shaking someone's hand without also offering the necessary full frontal body stance goes against our norms. Our instinctive memory bank tells us that one cannot be Accepted without first being Acknowledged. The incongruity will set off the alarm bells as well.

Unfortunately, this actually happens much more often than you might think.

A useful way to describe it would be to borrow a phrase coined by animal welfare specialist Dr. Temple Grandin: "The bad has become normal." Although she was talking about the horrifying state of conglomerate farm practices, it could just as easily be applied to the current state of horrifying communication practices (and many other industries where the height of achievement has been reduced to mastering mediocrity).

It's the glaring example of what is commonly referred to as "the photo op." We've all seen them: pictures of two people shaking hands, yet their bodies are both turned to face the camera. From their perspective, they are shaking hands at a profile, just as we've described. The result is that it both looks silly and goes against our norms. The whole situation rings false, and the Reactor (initially, the two people shaking hands and, ultimately, anyone who sees the final photo) knows it. Though we may ostensibly see Acceptance because they are shaking hands, we know that there is no Acknowledgment, simply because they are not facing each other.

So an act of cultural Acceptance must follow each act of full frontal Acknowledgment in order to progress the conversation, and you cannot have one without the other, or in the wrong order, without seriously disrupting our norms and setting off alarm bells.

As soon as you perform these two elements, Acknowledgment and Acceptance, in the right order, you have once again put in the proper Causes to get the desired Effects of these two steps, and the next door in your conversation will open.

When Shaking Isn't Practical

Of course, there are times when it is impractical, inappropriate, or impossible to shake hands with someone with whom you need to begin a conversation. Perhaps they are too far away, an object is in the way, or you are standing in front of an audience.

The best and only other acceptable way to indicate Acceptance is to first be sure you have Acknowledged that Reactor with a full frontal stance, make eye contact, then nod your head in her direction. A nod will meet the minimum standards of acceptance in circumstances where there is no alternative.

In the case of standing before an audience, you should face forward in a full frontal stance, make eye contact with someone right in the middle of the crowd, and nod to that person. Every other Reactor who sees that nod will accept it as the most practical norm available under those circumstances, thus satisfying the norm for acceptance for that situation. More on this will be discussed later.

You Have to Give Her What She Expects

Taking it one step even further, the kind of Acceptance we offer must be in line with what the Reactor expects based on previous history. Strangers greet each other one way, lovers another. The simplest measure of normal acceptance is to "pick up" the relationship where the last encounter "left off."

For example, were a teenage boy to greet his girlfriend in a manner more like they were having their first date rather than their fourth (maybe because "the guys" were snickering nearby), the girl would immediately wonder what had happened (her conscious expectation of the "norm"). Her intuitive alarm bells would go off and she would naturally question her previous understanding of their relationship. That spells trouble with a capital "T," as every teenager who has learned that lesson the hard way can confirm!

On the opposite extreme, it is equally detrimental to display a greeting in excess of the relationship. When someone we hardly know begins to treat us like we are old buddies, we immediately become suspicious of that Presenter's hidden motives, again, because it is contrary to our norms. Alarm bells will go off for sure.

Obviously, whatever the status of any prior relationship, as the Presenter, you must satisfy the needs of the Reactor's expectations by greeting her in a way your previous history together would dictate, lest the incongruity between your last meeting and this one create suspicion and disrupt the path to the next door of your conversation.

Finally, after all the handshaking, bowing, kissing, hugging, nodding, and any other physical greeting that meets the norm of the situation are accomplished, now is the time we can at last open our mouths and *say something*.

At this initial stage, saying something to meet the norms of the moment is easy. A simple "How are you?" or "Nice to meet you" is generally sufficient in a one-on-one situation with an acquaintance or stranger, and "Good morning/afternoon/evening" works fine for a group. Every culture has its own norm for the first few moments of greeting; you simply need to use the most appropriate one. Just be sure to use one.

TRUTH #5, then, is that you must follow your full frontal stance of Acknowledgment with a culturally accepted gesture of Acceptance in a way that will meet the norms of your Reactor in a one-on-one conversation. As for other venues, again, we will get more specific in later chapters as to how to satisfy those needs.

You *Can* Always Get What You Want

United we stand, divided we fall.
—JOHN DICKERSON

Obviously, up to now, it has been a relatively simple matter for a Presenter and a Reactor to Acknowledge and Accept each other, as our various cultures have made it fairly easy to progress to this point. The next step is to determine, as in Robert Frost's famous poem, which road you wish to take from here.

One road leads to a conversation that promulgates no further obligation or commitment to anything more advanced on either side. So long as all the cultural niceties are accomplished, everyone can get along just fine, though the conversation will only be cursory, with no end goal in mind. That is the road most often taken.

You'll recall that **TRUTH #2** shows that you, as Presenter, must determine what your needs are, to understand clearly what benefit you expect to gain from the conversation ("I want mammoth steak,"

"I want love and affection," "I want to be president of the United States").

We've also made clear that you won't be able to get mammoth steak or love and affection, or become the president of the United States without the help of others. When such help is successfully enlisted, you will have achieved the most important outcome possible in any communication: an Alliance between you and your Reactor. **Only through an Alliance can you ultimately have your needs satisfied.**

Therefore, the goal of every purposeful conversation is to achieve an **Alliance**. This is the road less taken, yet is the only road that leads to the satisfaction of your needs.

Now that we know we need to create an Alliance, there comes the task of figuring out what Causes you need to put in to attain the Effect of an Alliance. It begins by realizing that satisfying your own needs isn't enough. You must also satisfy the needs of your Reactor.

That's because the Reactor has no incentive to join an Alliance solely for the purpose of satisfying the Presenter's needs. That would be entirely unrealistic, no matter how persuasive the Presenter might be. In reality, no Reactor is likely to join a conversation, much less an Alliance, unless the benefits to her are made very clear. Her needs must be satisfied, too.

In fact, as we progress through our process, it will soon become clear that in order for you, as Presenter, to have your needs satisfied, you will not only have to satisfy the needs of your Reactor, you will have to satisfy the needs of the Reactor *first*, before you have any chance of getting your need satisfied *later*.

The good news is that you have already satisfied two of her essentials needs: that of being (1) Acknowledged, and (2) Accepted in accordance with the social norms. You have already gained momentum as you are approaching the fork in the road. By knowing in advance which fork you wish to take, and heading down that road without hesitation, you ensure that the momentum will continue, and the Reactor will be compelled by your actions to follow.

The easiest way to get her to come along with you is to figure out how the satisfaction of your need can also benefit your Reactor, then show her that benefit.

Let's say you've decided you want mammoth steak. You need help to shoo the mammoth in your direction so that you can slay it. You could offer to share the mammoth steaks with your Reactor. This alone might be enough incentive to persuade the Reactor to help you, and an Alliance would be formed. Good job!

Now let's say your Reactor is allergic to meat, and she doesn't want mammoth steak. What other incentive could you offer her to get her help? Perhaps she would like a new mammoth fur coat or a nice warm mammoth rug for her cave. It might take some imagination, and it will certainly take some knowledge of your Reactor, to discover what benefit she must receive in order to compel her to risk shooing the mammoth. Once you know what she wants, however, you have the makings of a mutually satisfying Alliance.

It should be obvious from this example that the astute and clever Presenter will soon realize that the most effective way to have his own needs satisfied is best accomplished by having the **Reactor's actions to satisfy her own needs be the very same actions that are necessary for the Presenter's needs to be satisfied.** ("By shooing the mammoth, you get your mammoth rug, and I get my mammoth steak.")

This is the perfect Alliance, the classic win-win situation. Though the Presenter and the Reactor can perform different functions and achieve the satisfaction of different needs (that is, the Reactor shoos the mammoth and gets a rug, the Presenter slays the mammoth and gets steak), both have their individual needs satisfied by the formation of this Alliance, because both contribute a function to that Alliance.

So, **TRUTHS #4** and **#5** are universally necessary for every conversation, and they bring you to the fork in the road. Once you've determined that you intend to take the less-traveled path leading to an Alliance, your first step after that fork is to activate **TRUTH #6,** figuring out how the Reactor can benefit from helping you satisfy your needs, so that you can propose a mutually satisfying Alliance.

Now that you have your intent and means fully delineated, it's time to get busy applying the next series of Causes in order to progress the plot. This comes from the actual content of the message.

PART 2

The Formula for Inspiration

Arranging Your Content for Maximum Effect

The object of oratory alone is not truth, but persuasion.
—THOMAS BABINGTON MACAULAY

in' spi ra' tion: to arouse or produce a thought or feeling; any stimulus to create thought or action.
—WEBSTER'S NEW WORLD DICTIONARY

The moment has finally arrived when you must consider exactly what must be said in order to get your Reactor to join with you in an Alliance.

As we studied the great speeches, great advertising, great sales pitches, and even great confidence games (also known as fraud schemes) from previous eras as well as today, and distilled them down to their most basic level, we began to discover a simple pattern shared by all of the best ones. We realized that regardless of the subject or the goal of the Alliance, when this pattern is followed, the Reactor is moved, is persuaded, is inspired to do whatever the Presenter asks. Once it is pointed out to you, you, too, will see how incredibly prevalent and effective this simple pattern is.

Here, then, is our Three-Step Formula for Inspiration.

Identifying with Your Reactor

"And yet," demanded Councillor Barlow, "what's he done? What great cause is he identified with?"—"He's identified," said the first speaker, "with the great cause of cheering us all up."
—ARNOLD BENNETT, *THE CARD* (1911)

Following your Acknowledgment and Acceptance rituals, the first words out of your mouth in every conversation must be a statement that will **Identify with your Reactor.** Your opening statement must demonstrate to the Reactor, in word and deed, that you are just like her, that you think the same way, that you share her problems and her feelings, that you experience the same things, that your view of the world coincides with hers, that you are on the same page, and that you have complete empathy with her needs, quite simply because those needs are your needs, too.

More specifically, as Presenter you must put in a Cause that will create the reaction of *agreement* from your Reactor, in essence, to give the Reactor something to which she can say "yes," and ideally, "Yes, I see that we are alike."

Consider that when you initially acknowledged your Reactor with a full frontal stance, the Reactor has already said "yes" on a small scale, simply by facing you in response. ("Yes, you have turned to me, so I have turned to you. We are equal.") When you further accept the Reactor with the culturally normal greeting, the Reactor has said "yes" again. ("Yes, I have the same cultural greeting, so this person is like me.")

As the content of the message becomes more specific, you must continue to encourage the Reactor to say "yes" at each subsequent level as we progress. Fortunately, once she has begun to agree with you at this preliminary level, the Reactor will quickly get in the habit of agreeing with you, and it will be easier to keep prompting her to say "yes" until an Alliance is formed.

Therefore, regardless of the circumstances, the venue, or the ultimate goal of the conversation, every presentation must begin with a statement that will invariably cause the Reactor to nod and mentally say "yes."

The simplest and most straightforward way to do this is to open your conversation with an *irrefutable statement*, a proclamation of information with which your Reactor can agree. By making an irrefutable statement, one that will be commonly accepted as fact, or at least is universally understood to be true, you will easily fling wide open several important conversational doors.

First, you will clearly demonstrate that you are just like your Reactor, that you have the same understanding of something, that you are able to identify with her, and therefore with her needs. It is the first step on the road to forging an Alliance together.

Second, when you are before a group of Reactors and every Reactor agrees with your statement, they are agreeing with each other as well as agreeing with you. This creates an immediate sense of unity among the entire group. This will prove to be a very useful attitude to develop in preparation for your ultimate Alliance. It is the beginning of establishing yourself as the leader, and this group of Reactors as agreeable and willing followers.

There are a number of effective and deliberate strategies for determining an irrefutable statement with which the Reactor can identify. Each can easily be tailored or combined for almost any type of presentation. Often, the purpose of the occasion easily dictates the most suitable strategy, though sometimes a bit more imagination is needed.

Irrefutable Statements

The Historical Approach
(or "That mammoth's been out there all week.")

The most easily recognized and widely applied method of identification is the use of the historical approach. Quite simply, as Presenter, you must indicate that you and your Reactor have the same historical background, a common history on which she can easily agree.

To use the historical approach, you need only begin at a point early enough in the story as to relate to a common denominator. Such a denominator can range from very current history (*"That was some rain we had this morning..."* or *"That mammoth's been out there all week"*), to significant, long-term history (*"Four score and seven years ago, our fathers brought forth on this continent a new nation..."*) Both examples illustrate the use of a common historical bond to which both the Presenter and the Reactor can relate to and *agree upon*. In this way, you can again cause the Reactor to say "yes," as in, "Yes, I can agree with that."

Logically, of course, the history being presented should be pertinent to the subject at hand. A reminder of corporate beginnings by a manager to his staff, for example, would be a sensible start to a presentation designed to redirect the future efforts of the company, just as President Lincoln's reminder of our common political beginnings was intended to reunite the citizens of the United States in a struggle to preserve the union during an incredibly divisive period. By depicting a mutual beginning, the speaker opens the door for a mutual future.

The Concerned Approach
(or "That mammoth looks dangerous.")

Another successful way to identify with the Reactor is to voice a concern or worry that the Reactor is experiencing.

Worrying is truly one of our favorite pastimes. It takes very little for us to start worrying about things we have never worried about before. Take a simple statement like "That mammoth looks dangerous." Though your Reactor may have noticed that the mammoth had been out there all week, she may not have previously considered it dangerous until you mentioned it. Now she will begin to worry about her security and will be in much more of a frame of mind to want to do something about it. On the road to your Alliance, this is just the reaction you want from her.

All you need to accomplish in this type of opening is to get the

Reactor to agree that yes, this is a problem, a concern, or an unsatisfied need.

Once the Reactor agrees there is a problem, a concern, or an unsatisfied need, the search for a solution arises. Naturally, as an astute Presenter, you only mention the concern because you have the solution, which you intend to offer at the appropriate time.

Of course, while this "worry" approach of identification can be quite effective, it is important to use it in moderation. When you pile worries upon worries, concerns upon concerns, the Reactor will soon feel the hopelessness of the situation and will conclude she is helpless to do anything about any of it. The result will be depression and no action.

In addition, when taken to extremes, this approach may also create the impression the Presenter is complaining, and excessive complaining becomes whining, and no one wants to form an Alliance with a whiner.

The most effective way to use this method is to identify only those concerns for which you intend to offer solutions, and discuss only those needs that you intend to offer a way to satisfy.

The Truth as We Know It
(or "That mammoth would make great steaks and a nice warm rug.")

This type of opening is an irrefutable statement that creates agreement simply because it is, in fact, the truth as we know it. "The cost of a college education is higher than ever before" is a statement of obvious truth, easy to agree with, hard to reject. It seems obvious, and the Reactor will likely agree with it readily.

Quotations
("The old wise man once said, 'It takes a mammoth
to feed and clothe a village.' ")

Using a quotation is another form of irrefutable statement. When you use a quotation, particularly when you give credit to whomever originated that quotation, you're making an irrefutable statement. It's a fact that that person said it, and whether or not the Reactor actually agrees with the statement, it is still irrefutable that it was said by the person being quoted; therefore, the Reactor is still compelled to say "yes." Ideally, of course, you should select a quote with which a Reactor can also agree, so that you can get a double "yes." Two for the price of one!

Whatever type of irrefutable statement you decide to use, it must invite agreement and be pertinent to the remainder of the conversation. Remember, the purpose of starting off with an irrefutable statement is to allow the Reactor to identify with you. It's the essential first step along the road to your Alliance.

Methods of Identification to Avoid

In reading the other public-speaking advice out there, we came across scores of lists of dos and don'ts. The lists of don'ts annoyed us to no end. The last thing we want our clients to think about is what *not* to do, as it clutters the mind and keeps them from remembering everything they *should* be doing!

Of course, it's the exception that makes the rule, and there is one exception where we are compelled to discuss the don'ts. It is because we must strongly dispel the many longstanding myths and old wives' tales that exist for this one particular element: how to begin a conversation.

Obviously, the first few moments of a conversation are critical, and many methods of getting started have been attempted over the years, with varying degrees of success. Making an irrefutable statement with the approaches we've just mentioned above will *always* work, thus they are a very safe bet.

The ones we describe below will work occasionally under the best of circumstances, but will fail much more often than not, so they really should be avoided. They are all strong cases for the idea that the "bad has become normal" when it comes to art of conversation. Here's why.

The Joke

By far, the most potentially disastrous—though often recommended—method for beginning a conversation is with a joke. There are even numerous joke books written just for that purpose. Have you ever wondered *why*? How does a joke, unrelated to the intent of the conversation, serve any purpose?

This myth originated as a shortcut way of trying to identify with the Reactor through laughter, since laughter is, indeed, universal, so theoretically it's an effective way to establish common ground. Unfortunately, though laughter may be universal, there are few human traits as disparate and impossible to predict as a sense of humor.

Whenever a joke is told, there are at least four distinct possible responses: (1) The Reactor could fail to understand the humor at all; (2) she could fail to find that kind of humor funny; (3) she could have heard the joke before (and may or may not have thought it was funny the first time, but certainly won't the second time); or (4) she can truly enjoy the joke. Obviously, the odds are significantly higher that the Reactor will fall into one of three negative and unproductive responses rather than the one positive response, which the Presenter desires. This is not the way to get a Reactor to say "yes" to your opening statement.

Further adding to the risk inherent in opening with a joke is the Presenter's potential lack of comedic talent. The old comic's adage "Dying is easy, comedy is hard" is apt, and Presenters are wise to heed it.

Of course, appropriate humor does have its place *within* many presentations; however, you must be extremely careful and use it sparingly. Telling a joke for the joke's sake must be discouraged for all except the most talented and experienced Presenter, and should almost *never* be undertaken at the beginning of the conversation. Few jokes are sufficiently capable of generating the kind of agreement necessary at this stage of the process, and will do much more harm than good almost all of the time.

The Question

Opening a one-on-one conversation with a question can be appropriate when we are speaking in more intimate settings. For example, "What's wrong?" or "How are you really?" and other such questions are usually suitable only for those situations when we are dealing with a Reactor whom we already know well.

When speaking to a group, however, opening with a question always has extremely negative effects. First, since most questions have considerably more than one answer, it is unlikely that every Reactor will agree with the Presenter. The chances are much greater that a Reactor will have a different answer from the one the Presenter had in mind. This makes an initial agreement between them, that essential "yes," considerably less likely.

Second, asking a question presents the Reactor with a dilemma. Should she call out the answer, or should she raise her hand? She risks making a mistake by choosing incorrectly, which would expose her as inadequate right from the start. What if she chooses one answer, then discovers the question was rhetorical? Again, there is the potential for her to embarrass herself. What kind of thoughtless Presenter would put his Reactor in danger of embarrassing herself? Certainly not one she would later want to join with in an Alliance.

Third, let's suppose the Presenter asks a nonrhetorical question with the expectation that his Reactor will give him an incorrect response. He uses that incorrect response in order to correct her, and to propel his conversation forward, but at the expense of embarrassing his Reactor. Again, why would a Reactor wish to join an Alliance with someone who has no reservations about embarrassing her in front of others?

Fourth, suppose it is a rhetorical question. It would be natural for the Presenter to pause afterward to give his Reactor time to think about the question, but for how long? How long before the Reactor begins to wonder if the question wasn't rhetorical, but in fact an answer is expected? How long before the Reactor becomes uncomfortable waiting? How long before she begins to wonder what kind of game the Presenter is playing? How long before she begins to think the Presenter is an idiot and she should get out of Dodge as soon as possible? How long before she realizes he's started speaking again, but she's been so distracted with all these questions about his credibility that she didn't notice and she's now missed everything he just said?

Wouldn't an irrefutable statement that the Reactor can say "yes" to be a more productive and straightforward way of getting the Reactor on your side?

Finally, and most important, asking a question during the opening of a presentation shows that the Presenter has no idea what the Reactor's needs and concerns are in the first place, that he apparently has done no homework whatsoever. If he had, he would know what to say to engage the Reactor, rather than having to start asking questions to discover a way.

This clearly indicates the Presenter's lack of interest in discovering the Reactor's needs, and will do little to encourage the Reactor to listen further. Again, until you identify shared needs and concerns, and are able to get the Reactor to agree with those commonalities, the Reactor will see no point in continuing this particular conversation.

Talking About Yourself

One of the most common yet destructive methods of beginning a conversation is to begin by talking about yourself. Though we mentioned earlier that the historical approach is a very effective way to identify with your Reactor, it is imperative that you as the Presenter understand that when using the historical approach, you must present a history that is common between yourself and the Reactor, rather than your own personal history. In reality, your own personal history is of little interest to your Reactor. Her interest lies only in whether or not you can satisfy her needs.

Nevertheless, many Presenters feel the overwhelming urge to provide their personal history, credentials, and past experiences in order to let the Reactor "get to know him," or to demonstrate his qualifications to speak on this subject. This is a serious mistake for several important reasons.

41

First, the Reactor is far less likely to find something in your personal history with which to identify than she would with a common history. When you, as Presenter, simply present a litany of your accomplishments and personal background (which we more appropriately like to refer to as your obituary), there will undoubtedly be a number of things with which the Reactor will not be able to identify.

Each of the items you list is an opportunity for the Reactor to say "no" instead of the desired "yes." "I grew up in . . ." (she didn't). "I went to school at . . ." (she didn't). "I've been married for X years . . ." (she hasn't). "I've got X children and grandchildren . . ." (she doesn't). Sound familiar? Like every political candidate's opening, perhaps?

Too many *nos*, *didn'ts*, *hasn'ts*, and *doesn'ts* soon leads the Reactor to think, "Who cares?" The biggest problem with opening by talking about yourself is that you have no idea how many negatives you might be provoking. It is way too dangerous. Once a Reactor starts thinking, "So what, who cares?", it's too late. You've lost her.

Second, talking about yourself, particularly about your own accomplishments, clearly demonstrates that your interests lie in satisfying your own needs, rather than the needs of your Reactor. While it is, in fact, ultimately true that you do begin a conversation with an eye toward eventually satisfying your own needs, the introduction of an Alliance must come later, and only after you have fully described the benefits *to* the Reactor, *for* the Reactor. Suffice it to say that few Reactors will be persuaded to join an Alliance with someone who appears to only be concerned with himself.

Finally, we all know that the most boring person in the room is the one who only ever talks about himself. Opening a presentation by talking about yourself has the same effect. Even if you eventually get around to saying something that interests or concerns your Reactor, it will be too late: She will already have made up her mind about you, and it will be that you are a self-centered bore.

On the other hand, by demonstrating knowledge of the history you and your Reactor have in common, you indicate to the Reactor the tangible effort you are making to identify with her, to include her as an active participant in the conversation. That will earn you another resounding "yes," and quite probably a bit of respect from the Reactor as well.

Starting with an Apology

It's surprising how many Presenters begin a presentation with an apology. It's hard to imagine why anyone would think this is a benefit to him. Let's think this through. You begin by apologizing that you didn't take time to prepare, or some other such excuse. What is the Reactor to make of that? Sorry you got stuck having to talk to her? Sorry you thought your speaking to her was of so little importance or consequence that you couldn't be bothered to prepare? Sorry you considered your presentation such a burden? Sorry you thought so little of her that you're willing to utterly waste her time? Sorry that you apparently know so little about your subject that great preparation was necessary?

Apologizing is just a preemptive excuse for the bad job you are about to do. This is definitely not the first impression you want to make.

Saying Something Shocking

Another commonly misused approach to opening a conversation is to say something *shocking*. Some people think this will get the audience's attention, a technique reminiscent of a teacher smashing a ruler on the desk to quiet unruly students. Though it may prompt a nervous giggle (which an ignorant Presenter may interpret as a good sign), in reality such a response is just a diplomatic reaction to the actions of an idiot. You must always respect the intelligence of your Reactor, and using sophomoric horror-film techniques simply doesn't cut it.

Beginning with the End

The final case of "the bad becoming normal" in presentation openers is the idea that a Presenter should (1) tell the Reactor what he's going to tell her, (2) tell her, then (3) tell her what he just told her.

This may be a method commonly taught for writing reports or teaching first-graders, but it is extremely ineffective for verbal communications (and not really that effective for writing reports and teaching first-graders, either).

Let's consider this "Tell 'em, Tell 'em, Tell 'em" strategy more fully. First, when you as the Presenter tell the Reactor where you plan to take her with your conversation, she *might* agree, giving you the "yes" you need. It is more likely, however, that she will decide she has no desire to go there.

The Reactor may believe, rightly or wrongly, that she already knows how to get there, or that she has been there before and has no desire to return. She may decide she has no need to go to that destination at all, and may just decide to jump ship rather than face such an arduous journey. In essence, the Reactor is allowed, indeed, even encouraged, to judge your presentational book by its cover.

Let's face it, if a friend invited you to go see the original *Psycho* movie by saying, "Let's go see *Psycho*. Norman Bates turns out to be his mother," would you still want to go? Would you enjoy it anywhere near as much without the thrill of the suspense? You can see how beginning by telling the Reactor the end is a very negative and counterproductive approach.

The only thing worse than telling 'em and telling 'em and telling 'em at the beginning is to continue with that approach throughout the presentation. By the time you've reached the final "tell 'em what you just told 'em," the Reactor's only possible interpretation will be that you think she is so completely stupid, she needs to hear something three times in order to get it. Why would a Reactor join an Alliance with a Presenter who thinks so little of her? She wouldn't, and she would very quickly want to beat a path out of the room.

The only function of the opening of a presentation is to identify with the Reactor using an irrefutable statement to get her to say "yes," period. There are countless words you can use to identify with your Reactor, yet ultimately, the desired outcome is always the same: to successfully identify with the history, concerns, and needs of that Reactor sufficiently to get the Reactor to say "yes." You'll know you've succeeded when you see nodding heads, increasingly attentive faces, meaningful looks between audience neighbors, and other indications of agreement. It's a sign she's decided to travel the same road with you. Once again you will have put in the Cause to get the Effect you want: agreement to your opening statement.

So **STEP #1** is to determine what irrefutable statement to use to get your Reactor to say "yes." The next step in the conversation will follow quickly and easily.

Introducing a New Idea

There is one thing stronger than all the armies in the world;
and that is an idea whose time has come.
—VICTOR HUGO

Having achieved the Reactor's "yes" to an irrefutable statement, you must now propel that simple agreement forward to the next logical step: the introduction of a new idea, or many new ideas. Bear in mind that new ideas are simply new needs that are only just beginning to make their appearance known, but will eventually have to be satisfied.

The easiest way to introduce a new idea is to make it the logical outgrowth of the type of irrefutable statement you used to gain the Reactor's initial agreement.

When you use the historical approach, getting the Reactor to agree to the situation as it has stood in the past or present, you then simply turn to the future, introducing her to the needs that she will soon be facing. As Presenter, you must simply make her aware of these forthcoming needs and ultimately provide her with ways to satisfy those needs. It is a natural progression that is very easy for the Reactor to follow and agree with. ("That mammoth has been out there a week. We should do something with it while we have the chance.")

When you use a concerned approach and the Reactor has agreed with your initial assessment of the concern, you need only introduce a new way for the Reactor to reduce or eliminate that concern. In other words, again, make her aware of her future needs and how to satisfy them. ("That mammoth looks dangerous. We should do something to get rid of it so we don't have to worry about it anymore.")

When making a statement that proclaims the Truth as We Know It, which should inherently deal with the subject at hand, it is a simple matter of progressing that truth from what we know it to be, to what we (the Presenter soon to be followed by the Reactor) want it to be in the future. Again, how to make things the way we want them is the same as satisfying a need. ("That mammoth would make great steaks and a nice warm rug. We have to slay it in order to get those things.")

Using a relevant quotation is much the same. ("An old wise man once said, 'It takes a mammoth to feed and clothe a village.' We should take the old man's wise advice.")

With every type of irrefutable statement, you can simply progress the current status of the statement in the direction you desire— toward your Alliance. Whichever approach you use, it should lead your Reactor to the same conclusion: "There is a need I must have satisfied, and I'm looking forward to hearing how to satisfy it." Having already agreed to the opening statement, the Reactor will naturally be swept along with the logical and appealing progression you have created.

Of course, being able to address the deeper needs of the Reactor is easier when you already know the person. ("I know she doesn't already have a mammoth rug in her cave.") But what happens when your

Reactor is a complete stranger, or when there are many Reactors to satisfy? Fortunately, this is easier than it may at first appear.

As we mentioned earlier, once one need is satisfied, it is quickly replaced by another need, and another, and another. This ongoing stream of needs is a constant, tangible, irrepressible, and usually indescribable urge that inhabits every one of us, driving us on toward survival. It often remains unlabeled and unnoticed, yet it is always there, always present just under the surface.

Knowing of the existence of this ill-defined and constant urge allows you, as Presenter, the opportunity to simply **inform** the Reactor of a definition or Cause for that urge. By providing that ever present need with a specific label, you enable the Reactor to see that previously undefined urge as an explicit need that remains unsatisfied, and she thus will have little choice except to agree with you that the need does indeed exist. Whereas your Reactor may have never considered the advantages of having a nice warm mammoth rug before, now that you mention it, it's a wonderful new idea, and by gosh, she needs to have one.

All of the best advertising campaigns unabashedly capitalize on first defining this undefined need, then providing the information necessary to obtain it, whatever *it* may be. In fact, whenever a producer or salesman convinces a consumer to buy his product, he is fundamentally establishing the same kind of Alliance that you want to initiate with your Reactor: Buy our product, and your newly discovered need (that one we've just now told you about) will be satisfied.

Of course, there are a few limitations to consider when setting out to define that need, such as that the Reactor must be able to readily believe that this need is indeed one that she could, and does, have. It would do little good for you to define the Reactor's need as a Harley-

Davidson motorcycle when in fact what she really needs is a minivan for her family of six. As long as your ideas are reasonable under the circumstances, they will generally be readily accepted by the Reactor.

So, **STEP #2** is to know what new ideas you intend to introduce, ideas that will satisfy the needs of the Reactor. Notice that we have focused mostly on the needs of the Reactor, rather than the larger need of the Presenter. That's because, as we mentioned earlier, the only way to get a Reactor to join your Alliance is to satisfy her needs *first*. (Patience, your turn to have *your* need satisfied is almost here.)

So now you have introduced a new idea, or new need, to the Reactor. The Reactor agrees that she has the need, and wants to have that need satisfied. Since every Reactor instinctively knows from her established norms that we never get something for nothing, you must now provide the information as to what the Reactor must do in order to satisfy those needs, just as the advertiser has to provide the information about how to obtain his product once the desire for it is established. This is the next and final step in our Formula for Inspiration.

Proposing an Action

We have to understand that the world can only be grasped by
action, not by contemplation.
—JACOB BRONOWSKI, *ASCENT OF MAN* (1973)

This is the final and most critical step necessary for the Presenter to
have his needs satisfied, yet it is imperative that he travel all the way to
the end of the road before taking this final step. Without laying the
groundwork to reach this point, or by trying a shortcut, he will become
lost or mired down, and will end up taking much longer to reach his
destination. Patience is absolutely essential to accomplishing the satisfaction of his need in the most efficient way possible.

Remember, we established in the beginning that you, as Presenter,
must begin with a very clear idea of what needs you intend to have satisfied as a result of your conversation. ("I want mammoth steak," or
"I want to increase my Christmas bonus by winning the district sales
competition this quarter.")

You also had to determine what you needed your Reactor to do in
order to have those needs satisfied. ("I need the Reactor to shoo the

mammoth in my direction so I can slay the mammoth," or "I need all the sales managers to increase their revenues this quarter so that we can win the sales competition.")

By following the steps to this point, you have put in all of the Causes to achieve the Effect of reaching this pivotal point in your presentation. Up to now, everything you have done has been toward the intent of identifying and satisfying the needs of your Reactor. Now is the moment when all of the groundwork that you have laid will get *your* needs satisfied.

First of all, it's important to recognize that we are a quid pro quo culture. Once you have introduced the new idea to your Reactor of how nice a mammoth rug would be, she understands that she is now going to have to give something to get something. That's the norm, and she's quite willing to accept that. After all, no one expects to walk into a department store and walk out with what they want without paying for it. Once she's decided she wants the mammoth rug, she'll want to know what she has to do to get it.

Now is the time for you to spell out exactly what price must be paid, what effort must be made, or what risk must be taken in order to achieve this ultimate satisfaction. ("To get your new mammoth rug, you'll have to go out and shoo that mammoth in my direction so I can slay it," or "To win the district sales competition, I need every sales manager to increase their sales by making two more sales call per day.")

Whether earning a bonus for increased productivity, paying money for a product in a store, casting a vote for a candidate, taking on the added responsibility of a promotion, or just reaching out to a friend in need, we all realize we must pay a price sooner or later.

Whether the Reactor accepts your terms for having her needs satisfied depends on her perception of value of having that need satisfied versus the price you indicate must be paid for it.

Caveat emptor: When the Presenter fails to disclose the benefits he himself will receive, or leads the Reactor to believe she needs to do little or nothing to get her needs satisfied, it will go against her norms, and alarm bells will (and should) go off. Criminals use these same techniques, so when an alarm bell goes off in *your* head, *listen to it*! Chances are good that whenever someone offers you something for nothing (or very little) you are about to be ripped off.

As with all free market exchanges, it is the Reactor who will ultimately determine whether there is good value in your proposition in accordance with her own needs. How well you identify and address those needs, and how "well priced" they are in terms of value for the benefit received from the Reactor's efforts, will determine how willing she is to join the Alliance. Should the effort or the risk appear too high in relation to the potential reward, the Reactor will quickly abandon the conversation for one that's more equitable.

Once she is convinced of the value—that the risk of shooing the mammoth is worth taking to get the mammoth rug—she will gladly "sign on the dotted line." Give her the paper and the pen and let her sign. Hand her the branch she will use to shoo the mammoth and tell her to start after the critter. Get her committed to the Alliance by asking her to do something, right now!

When the Reactor shoos the mammoth, you slay it, she gets a rug, and you get steak, the Alliance can be said to be a successful one, because you were able to inspire the Reactor to *act*, to *do something*, to *change something* that would not have been done or changed had it not been for the Alliance. This is the definition of **inspiration**, and the ultimate goal of every Presenter.

You must propose an action, and you must inspire your Reactor to take that action. That must be the goal of your Alliance, because it is the only way you will be able to successfully satisfy your need.

STEP #3, then, simply requires that you understand exactly what it is your Reactor must do to satisfy her needs that will, at the same time, satisfy yours. Then just ask her to do it.

So the **Three-Step Formula for Inspiration** is:

1. Identify with the Reactor.
2. Introduce a new idea.
3. Propose an action from the Reactor.

Every successful communication—that is, every communication that results in the satisfaction of the needs of both Presenter and Reactor—will follow this formula, one way or another.

More Than One Idea at a Time

When a conversation has several different ideas to offer, as many conversations do, the presentation of each idea should be arranged using the same Formula for Inspiration. As you introduce each new idea, you should preface it by identifying with the Reactor in a way that pertains to that issue, and follow the introduction by proposing an action, that is, what must be done to resolve that issue in the future. For each issue, keep repeating this Identify-Introduce-Propose pattern throughout the conversation. This will make up the body of your presentation.

These different ideas can be framed by an overall identification in the beginning of the presentation, and with a final, overall proposal of action to finish it off. In outline form, the presentation would look like this:

OVERALL IDENTIFICATION (Irrefutable Statement)
New Topic #1:
    Identify (Irrefutable statement on Topic #1)
    Introduce (New idea on Topic #1)
    Propose (Action necessary on Topic #1)
New Topic #2:
    Identify
    Introduce
    Propose
New Topic #3:
    Identify
    Introduce
    Propose
(Repeat as needed for each new idea.)
OVERALL PROPOSAL OF ACTION (The Close)

The Formula for Inspiration can also be used to create short answers to questions in debates, media interviews, and press conferences. It is the way to successfully arrange advertising. Properly used, a one- or two-sentence statement can, in fact, encompass all three steps in the Formula for Inspiration. ("There is a mammoth out there that would make great steaks and a warm mammoth rug. I'll take the steaks, you get the rug. Just come out and shoo the mammoth in my direction so I can slay it. Let's go!" or "Christmas will be here before you know it, and we can all have a big fat bonus and a trophy for the mantel just by making two extra sales calls a day between now and then. Let's go!")

This is the ideal way to arrange the content of every presentation of any kind, whether you are a keynote speaker at a convention, the best man making a toast at a wedding, an athletic coach trying to rally your team, an interviewee for a job, a politician making a stump speech or preparing for a debate, an expert providing an opinion to the pundits, an ad executive designing a marketing campaign, a law enforcement officer questioning a suspect, or even a parent offering advice to a troubled child. Any time you wish someone to do something, this simple three-step formula for content is all you need to create the inspiration necessary to get them to do it. It is the ultimate tool of persuasion. Please use it wisely and benevolently.

With your content arranged in the most effective way possible, we now know *what* to say. The next challenge is to know *how* to say it in an equally effective way.

PART 3

The Seven Elements of How to Say It

The Language of Your Body

There's language in her eye, her cheek, her lip,
Nay, her foot speaks; her wanton spirits look out
At every joint and motive of her body.
—WILLIAM SHAKESPEARE,
TROILUS AND CRESSIDA (ACT 4, SC. 5)

Now that you know how to fully determine and organize the content of your message, it is time to move on to learning how to create the most effective delivery of that message. For that, we use the greatest and most dynamic tool possible: ourselves.

When we begin to add the physical elements, which include our body language, eye contact, and gestures, we must do so again with the understanding that we must first determine what happens in a normal one-on-one conversation, in order to meet the norms that our Reactor would expect. Only then can we logically figure out how to make the same impression happen when the venue changes.

That same impression can only be created by using the technique of replication, putting in actions that will appear to simulate the actions of a one-on-one conversation in situations where that kind of intimate contact is more difficult or even impossible.

By replicating the actions, or Causes, the Presenter will also be able to replicate the Effects he wishes to instigate. Let's start at the beginning of our conversation, comparing each element as we already know it, then show you how to advance each element to other, more expansive venues.

Replicating the Full Frontal Stance

We have already shown you how the body behaves during the initial stages of a one-on-one conversation, that you must always begin with an Acknowledgment using a full frontal stance and direct eye contact.

When the venue changes and more Reactors are added to the conversation, the need for this acknowledgment is still there; however, the way to accomplish it changes, by using specific replicative techniques to create the same impression.

Imagine you are speaking to one person, and you are facing her full frontal as you should be. Now imagine that another person comes toward you from one side, wishing to join the conversation. Before long, you will be compelled to turn and welcome the newcomer with a full frontal stance of Acknowledgment, because that is the norm. Were you not to turn with an Acknowledgment, that newcomer would soon realize she was intruding, and sidle uncomfortably away.

When you are speaking before a group, the same thing must happen. As each new person joins in, you must, in turn, face each person **individually,** giving each Reactor as much of a full frontal stance as possible. Each individual Reactor must feel as though she has received the critically important Acknowledgment of a full frontal stance before she will feel she has been invited to become part of the conversation.

When you are speaking to a small group that has already gathered specifically to listen to you, you must remember that during the course of your presentation, you must at some point turn and acknowledge each Reactor individually. The sooner you acknowledge each one, the sooner they will feel as though you have invited them to join the conversation.

When you are speaking to a large group, however, it becomes impossible to face each and every Reactor individually in this way. This is when a replicative technique must be used.

Since you are unable to offer a full frontal stance to every person in a large audience, you must select just a few individuals to become a surrogate for the rest. The simplest way to accomplish this is to mentally divide the room into relatively equal sections, then select a focal point in the center of each section.

Imagine a triangle overlaying the area of the audience. Its base is across the front row, with its apex point touching the back of the audience directly in front of you. This will actually create three sections— one triangle in front, and a triangle on each side. Then select someone or something in the center of each section to become the surrogate to receive your Acknowledgment. See Figure 1.

Ideally, this person should be someone who will be easy to find throughout the presentation, perhaps someone wearing bright colors or that has distinctive features (President Reagan usually found someone wearing red, which is why the White House Press Corps wore so much red during his administration). That person will now become

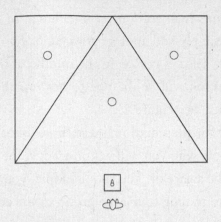

Figure 1. Triangulation of the Audience

the surrogate to receive the full frontal stance for everyone on that side of the room.

On rare occasions, when the audience extends much farther to the sides, it may be necessary to divide the audience into additional

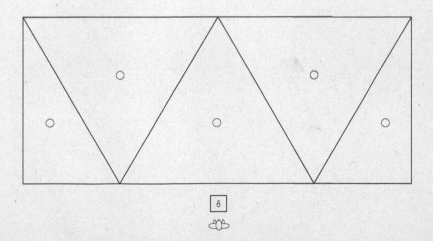

Figure 2. Extended Triangulation Map

sections, to insure each section feels included in the Presenter's full frontal stance. Simply add another triangle or two to each side of the mental diagram, select a person in the middle of that section, and remember that person will be the one to become the surrogate for the rest of that group. See Figure 2.

Throughout the presentation, these three (or five) focal points will be the only people who you will acknowledge, the only ones you will talk to or even be aware of. You should adjust your thinking from the idea that you are talking to a large group to the concept that you are simply talking to just these few people. That in itself will change the entire dynamic of your presentation for the better, making it much easier to capture the elements of a one-on-one conversation.

Replicating Eye Contact

The eyes are the window to the soul.
—ANONYMOUS

Eye contact is one of the most critical elements of a presentation, yet is the area where most presenters fail because of their own lack of awareness and self-discipline—awareness of the essential need for direct eye contact, and discipline for using a replicative technique that will at first feel completely counterintuitive, yet will ultimately provoke the same effect as it would in an intense one-on-one conversation. Using a replicative technique for eye contact is essential.

Before we can begin to understand the replicative technique, let's consider what happens in a normal conversation. This is one element that definitely falls under the Goldilocks Principle: Eye contact can be too little, too much, or just right.

The most common, of course, is too little. When too little eye contact is used during a one-on-one conversation, that is, when one person fails to meet and hold the eyes of the other for a long enough period to meet the norms, the impression created is that one person is uninterested or bored or dislikes having to communicate with the other participant. In the worst-case scenario, lack of sufficient eye contact can suggest that one person is lying to the other.

For example, how many times have you asked someone, particularly a young person for whom you are responsible, to look you in the eye when telling you a story? That's because we believe we can see the truth in the eyes of the Presenter, but to do so we must have direct eye contact for an extended period of time. (How long will be discussed shortly.) In reality, we believe we must have direct, extended eye contact with someone in order to determine their true intentions.

When too little eye contact is used, we can't help but feel that something is wrong. In fact, there's an old acting technique that teaches that when you want to look nervous, evil, or untrustworthy, you can accomplish it simply by shifting your eyes back and forth. The wider the shift, the more nervous or evil you can look. When someone unintentionally does it for real, of course, the same Effect occurs because the Causes are the same (think President Richard Nixon).

Of course, it's easy to make yourself look a person in the eye during a one-on-one conversation in order to avoid that shifty-eyed appearance. Trying to look **a lot** of people in the eye, however, becomes problematic. The more people, the more the problem is compounded.

Let's use the earlier example to illustrate. You're talking to one person when someone else joins you. The direct eye contact you had with the one must now be split between two. You start making less eye contact with each, and you start shifting between the two. Sometimes you can keep both involved in the conversation, but very often this lack of direct eye contact "disinvites" one's involvement, so the one receiving the least amount of eye contact will move on to another conversation that will provide more one-on-one involvement.

Should more people join the conversation, that eye contact generally becomes less and less for each person, with just a few words to one person and a few words to another, thus making it more and more difficult for everyone (or anyone, for that matter) to feel involved. Any semblance to a one-on-one conversation is totally lost by this point, simply due to the short time each person receives eye contact.

Eventually, when the group is large enough, the novice Presenter won't even bother to try to make eye contact with anyone; he will merely splash his message willy-nilly around the room. Now think about what his eyes are doing from the Reactor's point of view: They are shifting back and forth across the room, creating the very same effect as someone who is nervous, evil, or untrustworthy! The Effect is the same because the Cause is the same.

Sometimes, a more experienced Presenter (or a Presenter who has been told to make eye contact with no further guidance than that) will actually look for someone in the audience with whom to make that eye contact. Once found, he will deliver several words or a phrase to that person. Then he will become conscious of how many other people are out there, and will immediately leave that person in search of another person, splashing his message at everyone else in between.

As soon as he finds another person, he will again deliver a few words or a phrase to that person before he starts the process all over again. He may be convinced that he's making eye contact; however, from the Reactor's point of view, the shifty-eyed look remains the same. Eye contact for a few seconds is just as ineffective as no eye contact at all.

Finally, it must be noted that the same Effect occurs when a Presenter allows himself to be distracted by other activity or movement in the room. A good example would be at a press conference. Though the number of people may be small, making direct eye contact possible, it is typical that there is so much activity that a Presenter may find himself drawn to look at everything that moves. Each time he moves his eyes to look at a distraction, he again puts in the Causes to create the Effect of being shifty-eyed, with all of the negatives that includes.

Therefore, you must avoid using the "splashing technique" of trying to catch the eyes of everyone in the room, or allowing yourself to be distracted in a way that would create that shifty-eyed look. You must realize that direct eye contact, or the *appearance* of direct eye contact, is absolutely necessary to replicate the norms of a one-on-one conversation.

On the other extreme, it is possible to have *too much* eye contact. Too much eye contact takes on the appearance of staring, which, as we have all learned as part of our norms, is impolite and must be avoided. In certain cases, such as when you are doing a television or other broadcast interview, and you are alone and looking straight into a camera (often at the instruction of the producer or camera operator), looking *too* directly for too long will give you that "deer-in-headlights" appearance, which also has very negative Effects, because, again, it goes against our norms.

Fortunately, there is a simple and effective way to avoid all these negatives and get it "just right." We simply need to use some of the tools we already have at our disposal, and apply a bit of discipline and self-control. The results are well worth the effort.

Replicating Eye Contact with Focal Points

As we've said, it is just as impossible for you to make eye contact with every Reactor in a large group as it is to give everyone a full frontal stance, so there is no point in trying. Instead, you must replicate the act of making one-on-one eye contact to a single person.

You've already divided the room into sections. You've already selected a person in the center of each of those sections to be your focal point, the surrogate Reactor for all of the other Reactors in that part of the room. Now, in addition to having to give them a full frontal stance to acknowledge them, you must also use them as the focal point for your eye contact as well.

Naturally, the person you have selected as your focal point will know she is receiving your direct eye contact. As you look directly at her, however, an interesting phenomenon occurs: In addition to that one Reactor receiving your focus, many more Reactors both in front, behind, and even to some degree to the sides of that Reactor will all believe that you are actually looking directly at *them*.

This is what we call the Spillover Effect. Even though you may be looking at only one point, the Spillover Effect will actually create the impression that you are, in fact, making direct eye contact with nearly a third of the group, as shown in Figure 3.

This happy (and intentional!) side effect works for several reasons. Reactors within the proximity of each focal point are predisposed by virtue of their own ego to believe that you, the most important person in the room at that moment because you have the floor, are speaking directly to them. This is a natural human trait, one to be expected and

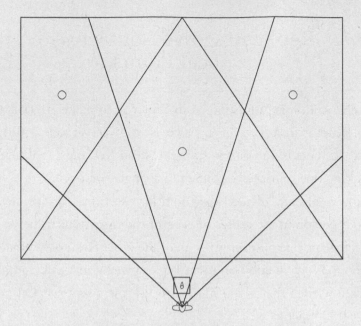

Figure 3. Eye-Contact Spillover

depended upon. Every time you look at the focal point in one section of the room, everyone in the Spillover area will believe the conversation is meant for her alone. Since you are acknowledging them with a full frontal stance by turning and facing that focal point, and then combining it with direct eye contact, the norms of a one-on-one conversation are being completely met by your replicative techniques. This will intentionally lull the Reactor into believing that you are, in fact, talking only to her (and everyone else is just eavesdropping!).

Of course, the effects of this vary to some degree depending on the size of the group and layout of the room. The larger the group, or the farther you are away from them, the wider the Spillover area. The wider the area, the more people will believe that *they* are the ones receiving the direct eye contact.

More important, by allowing you to focus only on one point at a time, this replicative technique eliminates the possibility of appearing shifty-eyed, nervous, untrustworthy, or evil, thus avoiding one of the most common and destructive errors a Presenter can make. In addition, it also removes any concerns you may have about searching for someone to make eye contact with every few seconds, a thinking process that often detracts from your concentration on the job at hand.

Finally, because you have disciplined yourself in the awareness that you are speaking to just three people rather than to a large audience, you will find it much easier to use all of the elements of one-on-one communication explained in this book.

The first time you do this particular technique correctly, the first time you truly connect with a person you have designated as a focus, you will feel an almost electric jolt, as though you have just plugged into a high-voltage electrical outlet. It may even disorient you for a moment, it is that startling. Once you have experienced this moment, however, it will be so exhilarating, you will want to repeat it. Perfect! Try it on your next focus, then your next, until it becomes second nature.

In fact, of all of the techniques we introduce to our clients, this simple understanding of connected eye contact is the one for which we receive the most gratitude. Even those who have spoken for decades without understanding this principle remark on what a difference it makes to them as soon as they put it into practice. It makes the entire one-on-one process seem absolutely natural.

Of course, this will work *only by maintaining an unwavering focus*. The moment you move off that focus, you risk creating the impression of being shifty-eyed, unless you know exactly where you are going from there. There are plenty of things that can disrupt your focus, and this is where the discipline element comes in. You must be disciplined to remain on the focus once it's established.

For example, should you look at your focus person and see she is looking elsewhere or writing notes or talking to the person next to her, you must resist the urge to leave her and look for someone else. You *must* maintain your original focus in order to create the desired effect of steady eye contact, for the benefit of everyone in the Spillover range on that side of the room. Should you waver in search of someone else, you've committed the deadly shifty-eyed sin again, and you're back to square one.

Frankly, when we're making a presentation, we take it as a personal challenge to get each of our focus Reactors to look back at us. Should we catch one looking elsewhere, we will continue to look at her, or even the top of her head, if necessary, until she finally looks up and meets our eyes. You'll be surprised at how quickly your Reactor can "feel" that look, and will respond accordingly by looking back!

Generally, you'll only have to do this once, and almost always at the beginning of your presentation. That's because once you are able to get that Reactor to look at you, and that Reactor realizes you are talking directly to her, she will be flattered to be singled out. She will begin to feel responsible for returning that attention (remember, we're a quid pro quo society), and will actually begin to remain fixed on you *even after* you have gone on to another focus. She wants to be ready for you when you return to her, if for no other reason than to not get caught looking away again!

Multiply that by the dozens, hundreds, even thousands of others who are in the Spillover area, and think you are actually looking at *them*, and you start to get an idea of the power of this method. Within minutes, you will have everyone in the room watching you as deliberately as the Reactor you are actually focusing on. This is how you earn the ultimate compliment a speaker can receive: "I felt he was talking only to me." When you get a dozen of those kinds of remarks after a single event, you'll know you've reached the pinnacle.

A Presenter with less confidence or experience, who fears that he will be unable to look at someone who is looking elsewhere, should fix his focal points on something other than a person's eyes, such as a bow in a woman's hair, or a man's tie, a forehead, or the rim of someone's glasses, whatever he can find in the right proximity. From a distance of about fifteen feet or greater, a Reactor is unable to distinguish whether the Presenter is looking in her eyes or at her forehead.

This technique will insure that if you as the Presenter fail to catch a particular person's eye it will have no effect on your concentration, eliminating another potential distraction for you. Remember, all those around that focal point will feel the strength of the gaze no matter who or what you are directly focusing on, as long as that focus remains as constant as in a one-on-one conversation.

By delivering your presentation to only these three focal points, in effect, nearly the entire audience will believe they have shared direct eye contact with you, and you will have had to share eye contact with only three people, thus successfully replicating what occurs in one-on-one conversation on both sides.

Other Benefits of
Three-Point Eye Contact

In addition to giving you a quick reference guide to where your eyes should be focused, the triangulation map in Figure 1 also considers another element of typical Reactor behavior—where she decides to sit when she enters a large room. Those Reactors with the most interest will sit up front near the Presenter; those with the least interest, or who believe the presentation will be boring and unengaging, will stay in the back. You need only think back to your school days to see examples of this, and to see why so many teachers are compelled to require mandatory rather than voluntary seating.

When seating is voluntary, those with the most interest generally elect to sit near the front, and are the most visibly responsive, with nodding heads and other signs of agreement, just as the Presenter wants. A novice Presenter will eagerly respond to those who are most interested, gradually gravitating more and more of his presentation toward those in the front few rows. Consequently, those farther toward the back will naturally begin to feel even more left out, confirming their initial judgment that the presentation would be boring and unengaging. Their *reaction* of disinterest becomes a self-fulfilling prophecy caused by the actions of the Presenter. As a result, only those in front will leave with their needs satisfied.

It's a vicious cycle that only the Presenter can break, and he can do so simply by directing more of his presentation toward the farther sections of the room, the ones conveniently located at the side focal points of his triangulation map.

By sticking to those three predetermined focal points, you can be assured that you are also reaching those farthest in the back. By focusing on those side focal points, you will unavoidably create the impression to those behind these points, that is, the ones farthest away in the Spillover area, that they are also important enough to be receiving direct eye contact.

By making the extra effort to include those farther back, you will be rewarded with greater levels of attention and engagement from a greater number of people. Few people are so inconsiderate that they would walk out of a room when a Presenter intentionally keeps trying to involve them. Once they're involved, you need only to follow through with the rest of your plan of inspiration to achieve your goals with *every* Reactor.

Even those few Reactors out of range of your direct eye contact or the Spillover Effect will be in close enough proximity to others who *are* to see their involvement, and will want to be part of the group, simply because of their instinctual need to be included.

With a little discipline, you will soon come to rely on the simplicity and effectiveness of establishing eye contact *only* with the focal points that have been predetermined. In this way, you can easily replicate the kind of eye contact that occurs naturally in one-on-one conversations, and clearly give the impression that every Reactor has received this most direct communication, even though you may never have actually looked at anyone directly. This is the beauty of the replicative method.

How Your Body Signals Your Intent

Now that we have established that we will be using a full frontal stance and eye contact toward three focal points throughout the presentation, we want to mention one additional subtlety, one that when mastered will add even greater strength to your communication. In some ways, this section will sound far removed from the task at hand; however, it is an essential building block to later steps, so you are wise to understand it fully before moving on.

Let us return to our gathering. Imagine you are having a one-on-one conversation with someone standing directly in front of you. Now imagine that a third person comes along. We know that in order for that third person to feel welcome, she must receive some signal from one of you involved in the conversation. Otherwise the newcomer will feel as though she is intruding and will likely move on.

Normally, you wouldn't want to break up your current conversation midsentence; you'd want to complete that sentence or finish making your point before turning to the newcomer. Yet you still want to let the newcomer know that she's next, and that you want her to stay and join in as soon as you've finished making that point. You know that if you don't let her know you want her to wait, she will leave, so you have to do something to signal that.

Fortunately, the human brain is always several steps ahead of its owner's mouth, so quite naturally, your brain will send the message to the rest of your body that you want to acknowledge this newcomer. The brain then lets the rest of the body know this Acknowledgment is coming, and the body will automatically begin to shift its weight in preparation for turning to face the newcomer.

Quite naturally, the newcomer notices the slight shift of weight, and recognizes it as a forthcoming Acknowledgment. She understands that you intend to turn to her as soon as you are finished with your sentence to the original listener. She knows to stay, that she is not intruding, and that, in fact, she will soon be welcomed, simply because you have shifted your weight in accordance with the norm.

Meanwhile, your eyes are still locked on your original listener and vice versa, until the completion of that last sentence or thought. Once the thought is complete, you are already in motion, feet first, followed by your body, and finally, by your eyes, to welcome the newcomer with the requisite full frontal stance and eye contact. Remember this order: (1) feet, (2) body, and finally, (3) eyes.

While this may seem technical at first, you must realize that all of what was just described happens in only a moment, smoothly and without thought. It happens so often and has become so deeply imbedded in our norms we seldom take notice, unless something disrupts that flow. When a disruption occurs, once again, our intuition sets off our alarm bells.

The most common disruption occurs when two people are talking, and a third begins to approach them, only to have the conversation abruptly stop, without the completion of the sentence or thought. What would the newcomer likely think? Chances are she would think they were talking about her, that the conversation had to stop quickly lest she overhear what they were saying about her. She would feel less welcome, even if all the usual required Acknowledgments had followed. Her alarm bells would take a long time to quiet.

So the norm is to complete your thought or point to one person before turning to the next person, and you can subtly telegraph your intent to turn by shifting your weight in anticipation of that turn. This is what happens in a normal, one-on-one situation. Anything that disrupts that natural flow of conversation between two, then three people, will result in the newcomer's alarm bells going off.

Now let's see how that applies when the numbers are larger and we begin to use our three-point focal system in order to replicate that same norm, beginning with the body movement.

Whenever we're working with a new client, a strange thing happens at this point in the training. Even though they clearly understand the concept of the three-point system and why it makes sense to use, when they begin to try to turn from one focus to another, something disconnects their feet from their brain. Their feet either get stuck to the floor and they turn only their upper body, or they have to take two full seconds to think about how to move their feet, as if this was the first time in their lives they ever had to turn to face someone. We know this sounds silly, but it invariably happens *every* time, with *every* client.

Now, you might think that turning to face people, something we do naturally day in and day out, would hardly need to be rehearsed. In training session after training session, however, when we ask people to turn from one focus to another, they almost always become stiff and unnatural, merely because they are thinking about something they ordinarily don't think about. For some reason it causes a temporary short circuit in the brain. Therefore, as strange as this may sound, you must practice until you don't need to think about it anymore, and regain the natural look you have when you aren't thinking about it.

Here's a five-minute exercise to get the feel of it. The first part of this will look and feel silly. Do it anyway; it will save time later, so just give it a try. Begin practicing by starting at your center focus. Now just for this exercise, lock your knees and rock back and forth between your feet, shifting your weight left, then right, left, right. Now turn your entire body to face your left-side focus and stop. You should notice that the last rock will be on your right foot, followed by your left foot planting itself slightly back in order to allow you to be facing your left focus when you stop. Move your left foot only as far back as you need to face that left focus with your entire, full frontal stance. You should now appear to be offering a full frontal stance to your left focus.

From that position, rock back and forth between your feet again a few times, then turn to face your right focus and stop. Once again, you should be aware that the last rock occurred on your left foot, followed by your right foot dropping back and planting itself so that you stop when you reach your right focus. Keep doing this back and forth between your two side focuses until you understand how it feels when the weight shifts between your feet.

Now unlock your knees and move your legs a little closer together. Instead of rocking simply shift your weight from one foot to the other, letting your knees flex naturally. You'll find this move will get your body doing exactly the same thing, only now you won't have to plant your back foot to stop; you'll simply be shifting your weight the way you normally would. You'll realize that when you are facing to the left focus, your weight will generally stay on your right foot, and when you turn to face your right focus, most of your weight will remain on your left foot. Do this between the two sides, three times for each side. Now come back to the center for a focus, then repeat to the sides a few more times.

By the time you finish this exercise, you should never have to think about how to change focuses, beginning with your feet, ever again. You'll also start to take notice of how people move naturally when they gather in small groups at social events, and that will help you to better incorporate your focus shift intentionally when you need to.

You should realize that this exercise has taught you more than just how to move your feet. It has taught you to move your feet first, body second, and eyes last, just like in a normal one- or two-person conversation. Once you get comfortable with your body memory in this way, it will quickly get in the habit of starting with the feet first without you having to think about it.

This technique is important to master before we add the next

n goes back to completing that thought before turning
focus. It also wraps into another element—determining
stay at each focal point.

Focal Time

Now that you have determined your specific visual focal points, and
have mastered the skill of facing each focal point by moving your feet
first, you must next determine **how long** to stay at each focal point,
and at what point to turn to your "newcomer."

Once again, imagine you are having a fairly intense conversation
with someone at a social gathering when that third person comes along.
How long can that conversation continue while someone is standing
there waiting to join in? How long before that newcomer realizes she is
intruding or is not going to be invited into the conversation? How long
before she decides to move on? How long before the conversants feel
they are rudely ignoring the newcomer?

We all instinctively know how long that time is, because it has
been established as one of our norms. Whether we are the conversant
or the newcomer, we know just about how long is too long, how long
before we feel invited or unwelcome. As an astute Presenter, you
must be even more aware of it, because that sense of timing must also
be applied in presentational situations.

Let's apply the above scenario to the three points of focus. When
you are turned to one focus, it is like having a conversation with one
person. The "newcomer" is your focal point on the other side. How
long can you remain talking to that first focus before you realize that

another person, that other focal point, is waiting? How long before the urge to include that third person becomes overwhelming?

That is the feeling, the sensation, the timing of which you must become aware in order to perfect your use of this system. As your awareness and experience grow, you will soon know from your own internal clock precisely when you have stayed at one focal point long enough. When the urge to include that newcomer becomes overwhelming, it's time to turn to your next focus. This is an immeasurably useful tool to be used both with and without a written script.

The amount of time this takes is what we refer to as a **thought byte.** It's a lot like the sound byte so popular with the electronic media, except that a thought byte requires a *complete* thought to be conveyed, rather than the limited phrase or two the media uses.

In general, a thought byte will be approximately twenty-five to forty words in length. If it is longer than that, the person left waiting may feel she is being ignored. While counting words can be a helpful guide, particularly for less experienced Presenters, it is important to recognize that it is the "feel" that matters most. It is more important to view the thought byte as just that—a complete thought—and turns to your next focus must be based on those rather than simple word count.

Putting the Pieces Together

So now we know how long a thought byte is, and that we must not wait longer than a thought byte before turning to our newcomer. We also know we must complete our thought byte to our existing focus before turning to our next focus. Logically, then, we should speak one thought byte to one focus, then speak another thought byte to another focus, and so on. At last, a pattern is beginning to develop! Let's take a closer look.

We mentioned earlier that when two people are conversing and a third moves to join them, there is a natural instinct of the one who is speaking to complete his sentence or point before he turns his attention to the newcomer. It is normal for him to complete that thought byte before changing focus, and everyone in the vicinity understands that.

Let's say he didn't finish his thought byte before turning. He simply turned in midsentence, saying the first half of his thought byte to his first conversant, and the second half of his sentence to the newcomer. The first conversant would realize the point must not have been very important or else the Presenter would have finished it rather than throw it away. The newcomer wouldn't have felt involved in the first part, so it would likely be entirely meaningless to her. Regardless of how important that thought byte may have been, it has been rendered useless by the fact that it was split between two people.

What's more, because the point was lost, and that goes against the norms, all three will experience a moment of discomfort that will strain the progress of the conversation.

Even worse, should the Presenter try to simply throw a phrase or two toward the newcomer during the course of his thought byte, he will not only disrupt the point of this thought byte, he will also take on that undesirable appearance of being shifty-eyed or nervous. Both the newcomer and the original listener will feel as though they are (1) unworthy of a complete thought byte, and (2) receiving this treatment from some shifty-eyed Presenter they probably want to get away from now anyway—direct Causes that lead to direct Effects.

All of this can be avoided simply by saying one complete thought byte to one person, right to the very end. Then, move on to the next person and say a complete thought byte to her, right to the very end.

Only then will both people feel they have each received the complete one-on-one attention they each believe they deserve.

As more people are added to the conversation or presentation, continue the same strategy. When in a small group, complete a thought byte to each person in that small group. Once the group reaches critical mass and you are using focal points, complete your thought byte to that focal point, just as you would to a single person in a conversation. It is the only way to effectively replicate the norms.

In a nutshell, when you turn to acknowledge a Reactor (person or focal point), you must also be giving them one complete thought byte before moving on to the next Reactor. This sounds surprisingly simple, yet when you see others make presentations who are unaware of these techniques, you will begin to notice how rarely it is done. When you compare them to those who do know and use these techniques, you'll soon realize just how much strength they add to the presentation.

Direction of Focus

When you are speaking before a group using your focal points, determining at which focus to look and when is a relatively simple matter, as it stems from what we have already discussed about where a Reactor chooses to sit. You'll recall that the most interested people will generally sit front and center, and the least interested will sit farther in back and to the sides. These roughly correspond to the three points on our triangulation map in Figure 1.

Quite simply, every *opening* statement should be directed to the center focus. Every *closing* statement should be directed to the center focus. Every one of *the most important* statements should be directed toward the center focus. Everything *else* should be split fairly evenly between the side focuses. Once again, there are logical reasons why.

Because the most interested Reactors are usually front and center, the Presenter needs to acknowledge their importance. By giving them the opening, closing, and most important statements, the Presenter lets them know they are getting the best bits, and they will have no discomfort that the bulk of the speech will be directed elsewhere.

Meanwhile, those Reactors at the sides will feel completely included because the bulk of the communication is being directed toward them. The directness of the Presenter's full frontal attention and eye contact will make it impossible for them to feel left out, and what's more, will encourage their complete involvement.

Now, let's put this all together into one example, by applying them to the Gettysburg Address. You will see that each thought byte is divided into roughly the correct length to make a complete point; each thought byte indicates which focus to use (right and left are interchangeable); and, though not relevant to this exercise (yet relevant to the development of your own message), the address follows the Formula for Inspiration of (1) identifying with your reactor, (2) introducing a new idea, and (3) proposing an action.

To Center Focus:

Four score and seven years ago, our fathers brought forth on this continent a new nation, conceived in liberty, and dedicated to the proposition that all men are created equal. (30 words)

To Right Focus:

Now we are engaged in a great civil war, testing whether that nation, or any nation so conceived and so dedicated, can long endure. We are met on a great battlefield of that war. (34 words)

To Left Focus:

We have come to dedicate a portion of that field as a final resting-place for those who here gave their lives that that nation might live. It is altogether fitting and proper we should do this. (36 words)

To Right Focus:

But in a larger sense, we cannot dedicate, we cannot consecrate, we cannot hallow this ground. The brave men, living and dead who struggled here, have consecrated it far above our poor power to add or detract. (37 words)

To Center Focus:

The world will little note nor long remember what we say here. But it can never forget what they did here. (21 words)

To Left Focus:

It is for us, the living, rather to be dedicated here to the unfinished work which they who fought here have thus far so nobly advanced. (26 words)

To Right Focus:

It is rather for us to be here dedicated to the great task remaining before us, that from these honored dead we take increased devotion to that cause for which they gave the last full measure of devotion . . . (38 words)

To Left Focus:

That we here highly resolve that these dead shall not have died in vain. That this nation, under God, shall have a new birth of freedom. (26 words)

To Center Focus:

And that government of the people, by the people, for the people, shall not perish from the earth. (18 words)

As this example shows, the correct time to change focus becomes apparent as soon as you break it down into complete points. The "feel" of the rhythm of the speech becomes unavoidable. Even those paragraphs with fewer actual words create the same sense of timing, since their importance, and the extra time they deserve, seem to fit right in.

When a presentation is to be fully scripted, the Presenter should realize that paragraphs written in accordance with the rules of prose or reports do not apply to the thought byte paragraphs we are referring to here. Thought byte paragraphs are generally much shorter than regular written paragraphs—as we mentioned, approximately twenty-five to forty words. Rather than counting words, however, the Presenter should base their length on how it feels when he says them.

The best way to understand this is to read your written script out loud several times, taking note of how "too long" or "too short" at one focus feels, and remembering our earlier example of the party conversation in which you are speaking to one person while another person is waiting to join in. Once you've determined the proper length, which your own norms will tell you, you should reprint your written script using thought byte paragraphs, as in the Gettysburg Address example.

This is also a good exercise for when you intend to make extemporaneous presentations, as the same guidelines apply. By becoming comfortable with the length of a thought byte paragraph when it is written, you can get a feel for the length of a thought byte paragraph when it is improvised. Practice will help solidify your "feel," until it becomes second nature and you no longer have to think about it. Remember, the less you have to think about elements of your presentation, the more closely matched to your (and your Reactor's) norms of communication they will become.

You should note that the changes to each of the side focuses can be either to the right or left, and the turn following the center focus can be either back to the same side you came from, or on to the other side focus. In other words, *vary* which side you are turning to when you come off the center focus. A Presenter who falls into a mechanical, predictable, and repetitious pattern, coming off the center focus to the same side every time, will soon have his Reactor(s) anticipating his next move.

In fact, whenever a Presenter does *anything* that creates a predictable or repetitious pattern, a Reactor will begin looking for that pattern, and will soon be so busy keeping tabs on that pattern that she will likely cease listening to what is being said. Too much watching and too little listening usually distracts the listener from the Presenter's message and could become a distinct negative. *Repetition is the enemy of naturalness.*

Again, be aware that in the beginning, you will have an urge to direct more of your message to those in the front and center, as they will appear to be the most interested. You must resist that urge. You must recognize that the challenge is to draw those in the back into your conversation, to get them as interested as those who are sitting in front, so that next time they come to hear you, they, too, will be sitting in front.

Having the proper "feel" for how long to stay at one focus, and knowing how to keep that focus throughout an entire thought byte, can come only through practice, though once you are in touch with that feeling, it becomes one of your greatest personal tools.

Now that you have a clear understanding of how to replicate eye contact with your Reactor by way of your three surrogates, you will find it relatively easy to apply when you are making an extemporaneous presentation. When your presentation is fully scripted, however, you must consider another challenge that involves eye contact: when to look down at the script and when to look up at your focal points.

Replicating Eye Contact When Using a Script

As always, let's take a look at what makes up the norms for this kind of eye contact. We've already established that you must make direct eye contact when you first turn to acknowledge your Reactor. We've also established that you must make sure you are making direct eye contact when you reach the end of your thought byte, to insure you've made your point and that your Reactor got it.

Now let's look at what happens in the middle. Whenever we say something, we usually begin in a reasonably strong manner, as we have been thinking about what we want to say during the moments before we start. As soon as we speak the words we had previously pondered, we have to start "thinking" about what to say next. Our brain skitters away from the moment at hand, and our eye contact becomes disconnected—in essence, looking inward at our own memory banks to figure out what we want to say next. In other words, we break eye contact momentarily. These moments of disconnection are essential, and in effect, are the most natural for humans to undergo. Therefore, that is our norm.

Once we've filled in the middle, we can now make a beeline to the strong point we had set out to make in the first place, and can complete our thought without further searching. As soon as we know the words with which we want to complete our point, we then reconnect with our Reactor by reestablishing eye contact with her as we reach the end of our thought.

Simply put, the beginning and the end of the majority of statements are the most important, and the middle is usually just a transition to put them together. The middle could be accurately described as "thinking time."

Unfortunately, what generally happens when a Presenter reads from a script is exactly the opposite. First, he will begin by looking down to find and read the first few words, which immediately prevents him from establishing the necessary initial strong eye contact.

Next, he will look up during the middle, less important part of the thought byte, usually to try to catch someone's eye so he can feel as though he has achieved eye contact.

Usually he can remember only a few words (because they aren't that important in the middle, anyway), and then he has to look back down to find the next few words. Depending on how long his sentence is, he may have to come up and go down numerous times before reaching the end of this thought byte. The more he goes up and down, the more he looks like a little bobblehead dog on a dashboard.

Finally, he reaches the end of this thought byte. In anticipating the beginning of the next sentence, he will look down during the last few words. Again, this keeps him from making the strong eye contact needed to conclude his point, and he goes out with a whimper.

The result—looking away from the Reactor during the most important moments and looking toward the Reactor at the least important moments—is diametrically opposed to the most natural way of expressing ourselves, and as such, immediately destroys the impression of a natural, one-on-one conversation.

Therefore, to be most effective, the Presenter must establish eye contact at the beginning and reestablish it at the end of each thought byte. To accomplish this when reading a script, we simply need to add another layer of technique to those elements we already have in place.

When using a fully written script, you already know where the beginning and end of each thought byte will be, so half the battle is won. Next, you need to determine how much of the opening and closing of each thought byte you can remember after just glancing at it; this is usually about four to eight words. You should then highlight, underline, capitalize, or in some way emphasize those phrases so they can be easily seen at a glance, as shown here:

FOUR SCORE AND SEVEN YEARS AGO, OUR FATHERS brought forth on this continent a new nation, conceived in liberty, and dedicated to the proposition THAT ALL MEN ARE CREATED EQUAL.

First of all, take notice of the proof of what we just established: that the beginning and end of the thought byte are the most important, and the middle is just words that get us from one to the other. In essence, Lincoln is saying, "Eighty-seven years ago our ancestors proclaimed that all men were created equal." While the middle words may be elegant and transporting, they are technically less essential to the point than are those at the beginning and the end.

As such, the underlined, capitalized phrases are the ones that must be said to your Reactor *with* proper eye contact, while the middle may be said somewhere else. "Somewhere else," in this case, is looking down at the script. Because the disconnect of eye contact happens in the same place as the norm, that is, the middle of your thought byte, your Reactor will hardly notice that you've broken eye contact with her.

Let's walk through a thought byte one step at a time.

First, glance down to the first group of emphasized words: "Four score and seven years ago, our fathers . . ." You should be familiar enough with this opening (on your own written script as well as the Gettysburg Address) that just a glance will be enough of a reminder.

Next, look up to your center focus (remember, the center always gets the first, last, and most important thought bytes), make eye contact, and start to say those words as far as your memory will permit. When you reach the end of those words (or your memory, whichever comes first), look down at your script and begin reading from that point.

Continue reading until you reach the highlighted end phrase,

". . . that all men are created equal." That final phrase of the thought byte (on your own written script as well as the Gettysburg Address) should be short enough for you to remember. As soon as you reach that point, look back up to your center focus, reconnect your eye contact, and deliver that last phrase.

It is imperative that you return to the *same focal point* that you left to complete your thought byte, so that one person gets one complete thought byte. Otherwise it would be just as ineffective and rude as saying half a thought byte to one person and the other half to another.

It is also imperative that once you look down within your thought byte, **you must not come up again until you reach your final emphasized phrase**. At first, you will have the overwhelming urge to want to look up every few words. Resist the urge! Though it may feel a bit uncomfortable at first, the advantages of this technique are numerous.

First, every time you look down at your script, it reminds the Reactor that you are reading. The more often you look up and down, the more often the Reactor is reminded. The Reactor will soon begin to think that you are unfamiliar with your own information, which will then lead her to wonder how well you know your own field or believe in your own message. This will begin to erode the confidence the Reactor has in your authority to speak on that subject.

Second, this up-and-down movement will detract from the strength of the sustained eye contact you are replicating. Remember, a Reactor is used to seeing a Presenter look away during the middle of a thought, and expects you to come back to her when you're ready to make your strong point at the end. By throwing unimportant middle words at her, you disrupt that norm and diminish the strength of your final point.

Most important, though, looking up and down more often will again create that shifty-eyed look, as chances are you will only be able to throw a word or two at your Reactor before you need to look back down to read. That, of course, conjures up all the negatives we've already talked about.

When the Reactor sees you look down, her mind-set will assume that you are looking down to consider that next important point, just as you would look away in an ordinary conversation. Even though the Reactor may consciously know that you are looking down to read, her mind will still sense that all is well and as it should be, just like in a one-on-one conversation. This impression will continue to persist so long as you avoid reminding the Reactor that you are reading a script, which you do when you constantly look up and down during the middle of a thought byte.

It should also be noted that when working with a camera for TV or other broadcast medium, you can avoid the "deer-in-headlights" look that too much eye contact creates by understanding and using this same principle. Feel free to look away from the dead-on stare of the camera in the middle of your thought byte, just as long as you begin and end there.

So, when working with a fully scripted presentation, begin at the center focus with the opening four- to eight-word phrase. Once you've reached that point, look down at the script and continue to read from it *without* looking up, until you reach the final phrase, at which point you look back up at the center focus and complete the thought byte.

The next step is to incorporate your turn, the one that will bring you full frontal to one of your side focuses. Here's where the earlier exercise will come in handy. Start by moving your feet to begin your turn to whichever side you decided to turn toward. If you did the previous exercise on page 78, this should be easy. If you feel stiff and unnatural or take more than a second to turn, go back and do that five-minute exercise now. It will save you much time and grief later.

As you begin your turn, glance down at the highlighted opening phrase of your next thought byte. That should take about the same time as it will to make the turn. Come up, make eye contact with your new side focal point, say the first phrase as far as you can, look down, read the middle of your thought byte, then come up to that *same side* on the final phrase.

Now start your next turn to the other side. Glance down to your next opening thought byte, look up and make eye contact with the focal point in that section, and start saying your opening phrase of that thought byte, as far as you can, then look down, read the middle of the thought byte (remember to stay down!) until you reach the final phrase, then look up and make eye contact again with the focal point on that same side.

Repeat this process from side to side, reserving only the most important phrases for the center focus. On a well-written script, that will occur naturally about every five to seven thought bytes, so the balance will be about two or three to each side focus before coming back to the middle. Remember to always make the final thought byte of your script to the center.

No doubt this method will sound a bit complicated at first; however, when you see someone use this method, the advantages become so obvious that you will want to master it, too. It will take just a little practice, and doing so will absolutely insure that you meet the norms in the strongest possible way, while avoiding the many pitfalls most Presenters suffer.

Eventually, with enough practice, a Presenter will become so adept at using this system that he will seem to have no script at all, because he will appear either to have memorized it or to be using only notes. This is an ideal situation for politicians or others who must regularly read scripts written for them, because when a script is prepared in this way, someone who understands the system can look extremely competent and expert even when working with a material they have barely seen. (However, reading it out loud a few times before presenting it is still highly recommended!)

So, after all this discussion, the key to understanding the second element of **eye contact** is simply to know that you must use eye contact (along with full frontal Acknowledgment) for one complete thought byte to each focal point, and the variations necessary between reading a script and speaking extemporaneously.

Now that we know what needs to be done with the plane of our body and our eyes, it's time to talk about one of our favorite subjects: gestures.

Speaking of Gestures

Our own physical body possesses a wisdom which we who
inhabit the body lack. We give it orders that make no sense.
—HENRY MILLER

Man consists of two parts, his mind and his body,
only the body has more fun.
—WOODY ALLEN

Few things can set off more intuitive alarm bells than the misuse of gestures. Few things cause a Presenter more anxiety than not knowing what to do with his hands. Few things can telegraph a liar as obviously as when his words say one thing and his gestures say another. Therefore, it is imperative that a Presenter fully understand the norms of gesturing in order to insure that those norms can, in fact, be replicated.

Every conversation begins when a Presenter forms an image in his mind that he decides he wants to share with his Reactor. To transmit that image, the Presenter commonly uses language and gestures. Both begin in the same part of the brain, that is, the imagination, then both get sent off in different directions to do the job they are tasked to do.

One direction (which we call the "word center") adds the words to the image, the other (which we call the "gesture center") adds the body language and gestures.

In a normal conversation, the physicalization and verbalization of those images will naturally coincide with one another. Your body will tell your story at one level, and your words will tell the story at another level. Ordinarily in a spontaneous and truthful conversation, both will be telling the same story, and their relationship to one another will adhere to our established set of norms.

Whenever there is a lack of synchronicity between a Presenter's physicalization and verbalization, however, those norms are disrupted, which sets off our intuitive alarm bells.

Naturally, in order to insure the necessary congruity to avoid suspicion and build trustworthiness, it is essential for your body to be telling the same story as your words. Let's see how that occurs in a normal conversation.

When an image is formed by the thoughts of the Presenter, and is then sent to the "word center" and the "gesture center" of the brain, the gesture center of the brain is able to act upon that image much more quickly, determining whether a gesture is necessary to convey that image, and what that gesture should be. When it determines a gesture is appropriate, it will immediately transmit that gesture to the correct part of the body to carry out.

At the same time, that image is being sent to the word center of the brain, which it has to come up with the right words and organization of those words, as prescribed by whatever language you are using, to describe that image in a way that will enable the Reactor to successfully capture it. Then the word center has to send those words all the way to the Presenter's mouth to be spoken, which involves a whole bunch of other instructions to the lips and tongue and so on. All of that takes a measurable amount of time.

The result of this process is that the gesture will actually begin to occur relatively far in advance of when the Presenter finally vocalizes that thought. Chronologically, the thought comes first, followed by the gesture, followed, at last, by the words. (Note that this is the same way human language developed in the first place. First the caveman thought, then he gestured, then eventually he made up some words to describe his needs.) This natural pattern

Thought-Gesture-Words

is always the same, and is our established norm for gestures.

Also in accordance with those norms, whenever the Reactor first sees the gesture, she experiences a moment of anticipation, realizing that this gesture indicates something important, something worthy enough of a gesture, is about to be spoken. The gesture, in effect, prepares the Reactor for this upcoming important point, and creates in her a sense of anticipation to receive it. Though it may take only a millisecond to register with the Reactor, that moment of anticipation is essential to meet the norms.

Whenever the timing or pattern of this Thought-Gesture-Words moment is disrupted in any way, however, its creates incongruity and a feeling of intuitive uneasiness. In most cases where gestures are concerned, this is usually a subtle discrepancy that people will register, but only register quietly. The alarm bells are going off, but most people who don't know specifically what to look for, or who aren't in tune with their own norms, will simply hit the snooze button, ignoring their own intuition. It is better to wake up to that intuition, because it is trying to tell you something.

Of all of the causes that can alarm our intuition, the improper use of gestures is probably the most predominant one. Again, following the Goldilocks principle, it's often a case of too little, too much, or just right, with the addition of unnatural and, the most common mistake, a gesture that occurs too late.

Too Little Gesturing

Too little gesturing very seldom occurs when a Presenter is working from the images in his brain, such as when he is having a one-on-one conversation. That's because the brain takes over and usually does what it is supposed to do, matching words and gestures to that image in accordance with the norms.

When a Presenter is speaking extemporaneously or using an outline, the images still originate from his brain, meaning the word and gestures centers are still intrinsically connected. Many Presenters feel more comfortable speaking this way, because it feels more "natural" to them, and so it is. Whenever a Presenter works from the image, the word and gesture centers will do what they are supposed to do, as long as the Presenter doesn't get in the way (which is another challenge entirely).

When a Presenter is reading from a script, however, he almost always falls into the trap of gesturing too infrequently. That's because in most cases, when the words are right in front of him, he takes a shortcut, going straight from reading the words to speaking the words, registering only enough input to insure he says the words as they appear on the page.

This cuts out the entire process of creating an image in the brain.

When there is no image to work with, there is no trigger for either the gesture center or the word center of the brain to kick in. The Presenter will cut straight to the words in the script, and simply regurgitate them without any image attached.

This usually results in words without any gestures at all, which is highly unnatural and incongruous to the Reactors' norms. Instead of Thought-Gesture-Words, the Presenter just delivers 0-0-Words. The Presenter will appear wooden and stiff and entirely too inanimate, and will fail to replicate a conversation in any natural way. We have all no doubt been subjected to this type of delivery, on a disturbingly regular basis. It must be stated clearly and for all time:

Words alone are never enough!

Whenever people interact, they use their hands and bodies to be more descriptive, and to insure that the important points are emphasized. It is a natural part of a normal conversation. Any observer in a restaurant, mall, or office coffee room will notice that people are always doing something with their hands and bodies, whether they are speaking or listening. There is almost *always* some motion, however slight. Attempting to make a presentation *without* including some gestures will immediately raise an alarm with a Reactor, as it is completely contrary to the act of a normal conversation.

Too Much Gesturing

Gestures create emphasis. In an ordinary one-on-one conversation, the gesture center of our brain limits the use of gestures to only those images requiring special attention. When the venue changes, however, and a Presenter starts thinking about his gestures, he interferes with his gesture center, overriding its ability to do what will meet the norms.

Sometimes a Presenter will overuse gestures in an attempt to force emphasis on images that do not warrant them. Sometimes a Presenter actually makes a gesture for practically every single word he says. Sometimes a Presenter is so consumed by making gestures that, as a result, the words get completely overwhelmed.

The problem is that when you emphasize *everything*, nothing ends up being emphasized—just as using cymbals to punctuate every single beat of a symphony would drown out the real musical climax. Instead, the constant crashing would only become annoying and overwhelming. Gestures must be reserved for when they will *add value to the words*, rather than overpower them.

Even worse, when a Presenter consciously tries to make more gestures than are normal, he will unavoidably begin to repeat some gestures over and over (think President George H. W. Bush and his karate chop gesture). Just as a Presenter would lose all credibility by repeating the same words over and over again (like an annoying talking parrot with a limited vocabulary, or an exaggeratedly annoying character in a *Saturday Night Live* sketch), so, too, does he lose credibility when he repeats the same gesture over and over again.

Remember, *repetition is the enemy of naturalness*. Whether it is in gestures, body movement, eye contact, or any other element of presentation, it is an enemy that must be avoided, as it will inevitably become a distraction to the Reactor. Whenever a Reactor begins to notice something she sees or hears being repeated over and over, she will start to anticipate it. That means she is spending so much time looking for the next occurrence of that phrase or action, she will be too distracted to listen or react to the rest of what the Presenter is saying or doing.

Gesturing Too Late

More often and more disturbing is when a gesture arrives late. This happens when the gesture arrives at the same time or after the words are being said. During a one-on-one conversation, a natural gesture will always come *before* the words (remember the natural order—Thought-Gesture-Words), and anything other than that will disrupt the norms.

When a Presenter starts to think about his gestures, that is, when and where he wants to place them for emphasis (usually because he's been told, with no further guidance, that he must gesture), he again disrupts his gesture center's ability to function in a normal way.

Remember, in a one-on-one conversation, a Presenter will see the image, which naturally goes to his gesture and word centers, which will then do their respective jobs. Let's assume that the image is one that the gesture center decides isn't important enough to add an image to, so it doesn't send the body any instructions to do anything.

Now let's say the Presenter has decided he wants to force a gesture with that image. He will have the same initial image in his mind, but just after he sees that image he will remember that he has decided he wants to gesture with that image, so he instructs his gesture center to add a certain planned gesture—in essence, mentally telling himself, "Gesture here."

Unfortunately, that second thought would obviously occur *after* the original image. By the time the body gets the message, the words that the gesture was supposed to accompany have *long* passed. At best, the gesture might come out at the same time as the words, but in any event, it will not precede the words as it should when done in accordance with the norm.

The result is that instead of Thought-Gesture-Words, it becomes Thought-Words-Gesture. This momentary disturbance in the natural flow of things will invariably and inevitably cause the gesture to be late, which is sufficient to register as incongruous to the Reactor.

The same disruption will occur when a gesture takes place at the *same time* as the words, which happens whenever a Presenter rehearses a planned gesture, believing that the way to emphasize certain words is to gesture at the exact same moment that those words are spoken. Suffice it to say, the effects are just as incongruous, and will set off the alarm bells just as surely as when the gesture is late.

There is one additional instance when a Presenter's gestures arrive too late: when he is lying or in some way being untruthful. That is because the first image in a Presenter's mind will be the truth, which will then be passed along to the gesture and word centers of the brain. The gesture center of the brain will begin to instruct the body to do what is necessary to describe that image. Meanwhile, the Presenter realizes that he doesn't want to describe that image quite in that way, so he pauses and takes the opportunity to craft words that are contrary to that corresponding image. To the astute observer, the body will be saying one thing while the words say another.

Even when a liar tries to change his gestures to match his lie, it's always too late because the gesture center won't be getting the message of the revised image until after the lie is well on its way to his mouth. Therefore, the gesture designed to correspond with a lie will always come after the lie.

Close scrutiny of the recording of a certain president when he stated, "I did not have sex with that woman," clearly reveals the finger pointing gesture that accompanied that disclaimer was far too late to meet the norms of the truth. So, too, was the same gesture late when it was used by a certain baseball player who declared before a Congressional hearing, "I have never knowingly used steroids in my life." Watch any Dennis Hopper movie and you'll see the tardiness of his gestures on nearly everything he says, a rarity in a professional presenter, as most actors learn early that gestures must always come first to appear natural (though it might explain why he is almost always typecast as a bad guy). It's obvious once you know what to look for, and few liars are good enough to overcome it (though some are, so beware!).

To be natural and to meet the norms of the Reactor, a gesture must always occur *before* the words, albeit only milliseconds before. It must always occur in the Thought-Gesture-Words order to meet the norm.

It should also be noted that the more important the point, the earlier the gesture tends to naturally occur. The Presenter should understand that a gesture creates anticipation, and when an important point is going to be made, creating anticipation by using an early gesture is one sure way of knowing it will get the attention it deserves.

Unnatural Gestures

Finally, as you become more attuned to the nature of gestures and how they are most commonly used and misused, you'll start to notice some additional peculiar choices ineffective Presenters often make.

For example, sometimes a Presenter will decide to demonstrate the size and shape of something by using his hands in a very exacting way, like forming a square or circle or box. Unfortunately, this inevitably ends up looking as contrived as it sounds. For starters, in normal conversation few people make specific movements when they gesture unless it is absolutely integral to the point being emphasized. What's more, these overly specific and distracting gestures often come at the same time as the words, rather than preceding the words, which adds to the jarring and unnatural effect.

That's because, again, when you try to plan exactly where a gesture should be, it doesn't originate from the image, it originates from a subsequent instruction from the Presenter. Therefore, it will always be out of the natural order, as the gesture will correspond with the directive rather than the initial image.

Other forms of unnatural gestures are those that would simply never be made in a normal conversation. The karate chop that President George H. W. Bush was so fond of using is one example, the knuckle point used by Senator John Kerry during the 2004 presidential campaign another. During a presentation, when you see someone using a gesture that you've never seen used in a normal conversation, then you know that Presenter is unable to figure out what to do with his hands, so he makes up a gesture and keeps inserting it whenever he tells himself to gesture (which is usually in the wrong place, anyway).

So not only is the Presenter using an unnatural gesture in all the wrong places, he is also repeating the same gesture over and over again. As was mentioned, **repetition is the enemy of naturalness**, so it shouldn't surprise anyone that these repetitious gestures get ridiculed by comedians and even everyday people. They look ridiculous, and should be avoided.

For the truly astute observer, here's another way to "read" a Presenter's gestures that's fun to watch for: its physical origination point.

When a Presenter's gesture comes naturally, as it does during a normal one-on-one conversation, the movement will always originate from the center of the body. In other words, a natural hand gesture will begin at the shoulder and move outward through the elbow and wrist, before arriving at the intended gesture point, the fingertips, and beyond.

When a gesture originates as the result of a Presenter consciously telling himself to gesture, only that single part of the body instructed to gesture will actually move. A Presenter telling his hand to move will only move his hand. Everything in between—the shoulder, elbow, and wrist—will be excluded from the move, since only the hand received the instruction from the brain. This results in a very stiff and unnatural-looking gesture.

The natural gesture, then, originates from the center of the body and moves outward. An unnatural gesture originates at the same place as the end gesture (starts at the hand, ends at the hand), and has a complete lack of movement of all the parts in between. Needless to say, gestures that originate away from the body and go nowhere can be easily spotted by the Reactor as false and insincere. Alarm bells will be ringing.

Natural Gestures

Regardless of how deeply one wishes to go into the details of gesturing, ultimately, it is the incongruity or lack of synchronicity between the gestures and words that causes the Reactor's intuitive alarm bells to go off. Any Reactor will soon become suspicious of a Presenter whose words and body language appear to be saying two different things. This is why the appropriate use of gestures is so critical to the Presenter.

Obviously, there are far too many things to think about when determining when and how to gesture during a presentation. Trying to do so is impossible, and would distract you from the job at hand. As we mentioned earlier, the more you think, the further you will stray from the norms; therefore, the less thinking you have to do, the better. Remember this: "When you think, you stink."

Fortunately, there is a simple and effective technique that addresses all of these concerns and is the key to mastering gestures. Simply stated, whenever you have an overwhelming, almost uncontrollable *need* to gesture, give yourself the freedom to do so. No attempt to stop gestures should be made, and no attempt to make gestures should be made.

You should never think about *when* you should gesture. Yet you should be fully comfortable in the knowledge that you have the freedom to when the urge becomes overwhelming. When the image is strong enough and the point important enough, your gesture center will automatically provide the uncontrollable urge to gesture, as well as the appropriate gesture to express that image.

The best rule of thumb for gestures is simply to just *wait for it*, then when you feel it, *go for it!* Eventually, with experience, you will never need to consciously think about your gestures again.

With a strong understanding of the norms of the physical elements of gestures, eye contact, and a full frontal stance, we can now move on to the most colorful and creative aspect of a one-on-one conversation: vocalization.

The Living Voice

The living voice is that which sways the soul.
—PLINY THE YOUNGER

He ceased; but left so pleasing on their ear his voice, that
listening they seemed to hear.
—ALEXANDER POPE

A speech is poetry: cadence, rhythm, imagery, sweep!
A speech reminds us that words, like children, have the power
to make dance the dullest beanbag of a heart.
—PEGGY NOONAN

In addition to the body language that accompanies the Presenter's words, the *way* something is said, its pitch, pace, tone, volume, and variety, is perhaps even more important than *what* is being said. Long before we learn the meaning of words, we understand the *intent* of a communication simply by the way it is vocalized.

The gibberish that a parent coos to a baby may technically mean nothing, but the *intent* of that message, to soothe and comfort, or to warn and protect, is extremely clear to the infant Reactor. She can receive a clear image even without understanding the actual meaning of the words.

Once we have a vocabulary, we also learn that the meaning of words can often vary according to the *way* something is vocalized. To a teenager, there is a distinct difference between the loud, harsh **"No!"** expressed by a waiting-up-late father than the more subdued, room-for-change *"No . . ."* they might get from an early-morning "happy you made it home last night" mother.

Once again, despite the countless vocal variations available to us, we accumulate enough experience with it during the early part of our lifetime to establish a vocal norm. This limitless variety is such that, it is, in fact, the *lack* of variety that causes us the most difficulty when a conversation turns into a presentation.

Fortunately, vocalization is by far the most versatile, flexible, and effective element you can master. Even small changes in your vocalization can create major changes in the response of your Reactor. When all other factors are equal, vocalization will make the greatest impact on your Reactor.

A Presenter has many factors to consider when he wishes to replicate the most natural-sounding vocal patterns. Before learning how to do so, however, it is essential to understand an even more important (and even less often considered) factor: the value of silence.

Learn to Love
the Pause

Listen to the sounds of silence . . .
—SIMON & GARFUNKEL

The right word may be effective, but no word was ever as
effective as a rightly timed pause.
—MARK TWAIN

Very few actions will get your Reactor's attention faster or more completely than the use of a well-placed pause. A moment of intentional, active silence creates the most dynamic, deliberate reaction you could ever hope to achieve.

In a normal one-on-one conversation, pauses occur quite naturally. Sometimes those pauses occur as a moment of thinking time for the Presenter. The more thinking time the Presenter uses, the more the Reactor will believe that the Presenter is sorting through his reams of knowledge in order to make sure he has selected precisely the correct words to use to make an (apparently) very important point. This will earn the Reactor's respect of the Presenter for delivering such a carefully thought-out message. Therefore, the longer the pause—indicating the longer the thinking time—the more impressed the Reactor will be.

Sometimes pauses are used to get the Reactor's attention. Remember during your school days, how if someone was talking out of turn, the quickest way to shut them up was for the teacher to stop talking? It took only a few moments of silence from the teacher before the culprits would be compelled to turn their attention back to the teacher (though usually after a few moments of uncomfortably squirming in their seats). A momentary pause is a surefire way to capture your Reactor's attention.

Sometimes a pause is used to create anticipation. When you are telling a story and want to create suspense, build an expectation to the climax, or telegraph that you are about to reach the punchline in a joke, nothing works better. The longer the pause, the more anticipation you build.

An extreme example of using a pause to build anticipation is found in the speaking techniques of Adolf Hitler, arguably the greatest, most effective orator of the twentieth century. When he addressed crowds numbering in the hundreds of thousands at stadiums throughout Germany, he would often begin by stepping out on the platform, then staring up to the heavens as though for divine inspiration. He would remain silent, sometimes for as long as seven or eight minutes, never looking at the crowd, never saying a word. Gradually, the crowd would become quieter and quieter, until it was absolutely silent. Imagine 100,000-plus people in an outdoor stadium absolutely silent! Only then would Hitler begin. Is it any wonder he was often accused of hypnotizing his audiences? Yet he was only using his understanding of the norms of his Reactors, and their predictable response to a pause, for his own nefarious purposes.

As you can see, long pauses, when properly placed, are an extraordinarily formidable element to understand. The longer the pause, the more anticipation is built, and the more attention your Reactor will pay to whatever comes next.

The Pause Filler

Whether it is a one-on-one conversation or a presentation before a group, many Presenters wrongly believe that pauses are the antithesis of speaking and, therefore, must be avoided at all costs. They fear that any hesitation will be seen as an indication that they are unable to think of what to say next, thus exposing a lack of knowledge or, even worse, a shirking of their responsibility to speak. In cases of public speaking, the Presenter often has the unfortunate mind-set that he has been brought in to *speak*, and speak he will, come hell or high water!

The unfortunate result is that any time a pause seems imminent (the kind of pause a Presenter would normally use to think about what he wants to say next), the compulsion of the misguided is to fill that pause with what we refer to as "pause fillers."

Pause fillers are those irritating noises that come out of a person's mouth when they are "thinking." They are the "ums," "uhs," and "ya knows" that are taking over the conversational and presentational landscape, a cacophony of noises that seem to pervade many presentations from the beginning to the bitter end. Even professional broadcasters and those who make their living speaking, such as politicians, pundits, and so-called experts in their fields, seem to have become mired in this annoying habit. Pause fillers, not pauses, are the true antithesis to speaking.

Think about it. When you hear someone verbalize his thinking time, doesn't that actually call attention to his lack of knowledge? When it happens repeatedly, does it make you think he has more knowledge, or less? Do you feel he is more informed, or less? Does he seem more intelligent, or less? Would you want to become part of an Alliance with someone who seems unable to make his message clear?

Now imagine that instead of all those uhs, ums, and ya knows, you are treated to a pause, a cool, clear moment of silence in which you can fully appreciate the image the Presenter just left with you. Hear it? . . . The wonderful sound of silence? . . . Now isn't that better?

Rather than giving the appearance of not being able to think of something to say, pausing actually provides the benefit of making it appear as though the Presenter is sorting through reams of knowledge in order to carefully select just the right words to convey his image. Where ums and uhs make it sound like the Presenter is scrambling, a pause makes it sound like he is being conscientious and taking great care so that the Reactor receives a clear and concise image.

Because these pause fillers actually call more attention to the Presenter's apparent lack of knowledge, he will actually appear to be ignorant of the very subject on which he speaks. Any authority he may have established by his credentials or the content of the presentation will be diminished. It will be easy for the Reactor to conclude that the Presenter knows less on the subject than she does and that, therefore, none of her needs on the subject can be satisfied by him. Thus the conversation becomes pointless.

Worse, when a Presenter constantly fills in his gaps with "ya knows," he comes across as actually *apologizing* to the Reactor for bothering her with stuff she already knows anyway. A Presenter should never apologize for being a Presenter, for it destroys all credibility and any chance of a future Alliance. These pause-filling nonwords become extremely bad habits that every Presenter should break as soon as possible.

One way to do so is to listen for them in others, and every time you hear someone say, "Ya know," you should mentally add the tag, "Yeah, I *do* know, so why are you telling me!?" Eventually, the tag will become such a habit to you that you will be unable to use these filler words yourself without your brain adding the tag and, sooner or later, you will cut down or, ideally, eliminate their use.

The Power of a Pause

By replacing these "pause fillers" with a simple moment of silence, however, the Presenter will instill in the Reactor a feeling of anticipation. The Presenter can use a moment of suspense integral to his story, or to make sure he has everyone's attention. In either case, the Reactor will understand that what is about to follow is extremely important. *The longer the pause, the more the anticipation builds.* When the message appears to be *that* important to the Presenter, the Reactor is much more compelled to believe it will be important to her as well. She will wait with bated breath for the Presenter to speak.

Of course, as with every other presentational element, it's possible to overdo it. While most Presenters underuse pauses, a few at the other end of the spectrum seem to pause after *every* statement. Just like gesturing for every statement or repeating the same phrase over and over, using too many pauses destroys their value. **Trying to create emphasis on everything results in emphasis on nothing.**

A successful pause is one that heightens the Reactor's anticipation for the statement that is to follow. Anyone who has ever listened to the great Paul Harvey on the radio anytime during the last eight decades has heard a master of the pause.

By now, you should certainly realize that rather than being the antithesis of speaking, **pauses** are actually an integral and critical element of your conversation, and well worth taking the time to learn to use effectively. To be an outstanding Presenter, you must learn to *love the pause*!

Pauses are simply the space we put between images, both the images we create as a Presenter and the images that the Reactor receives from us. To better understand how to use pauses most effectively, it helps to understand a bit more about the process of imagination.

Thoughts and Images

Picture yourself on a boat on a river . . .
—THE BEATLES

If you can dream it, you can do it.
—ALBERT EINSTEIN

The empires of the future are the empires of the mind.
—WINSTON CHURCHILL

Though science has made tremendous leaps toward understanding the workings of the brain, much is still unknown. One of the things most scientists do agree on, however, is that the uniqueness of the human brain lies in its ability to imagine.

Imagination allows us to project a situation into the future. Imagination compels us to use symbols such as the alphabet and numbers in order to comprehend intangible ideas. And imagination that can trigger a tremendous human emotional reaction from a simple, private thought. All these are made possible by the illusionary pictures in our mind.

As we said earlier, communication is simply the transfer of an image from the Presenter's mind into the Reactor's. It begins with a thought that formulates the image, then moves out from there to the gesture and word centers of the brain, in our Thought-Gesture-Word pattern.

The Reactor responds to that image in a different order. She will (1) see the gesture, which will create anticipation of the words, (2) hear the words, then (3) create a symbolic image of what the words and gestures mean to her.

Then there are two added steps: (4) She must further correlate how that thought relates to her own previous images of that thought, determining how she feels about it and whether she agrees or disagrees with it. Once she has formulated an opinion about that thought, she can then finally (5) file that new image wherever it belongs in the brain. That can range anywhere from the round file to be quickly forgotten, or the Things To Do file to be done at once.

As lightning fast as the brain may be, the process of steps 1 through 5 still takes a perceptible amount of time. When a Presenter depicts images that are familiar to the Reactor, these steps will take relatively less time. When the image is one the Reactor has never before considered, she must conjure up a completely new, symbolic image from scratch. This will take considerably more time.

This time to create images, of course, conveniently occurs during the **pauses** provided by you, the Presenter. The more important the image or description, or the farther that image is from what the Reactor already knows, the more time is necessary for that image to be clearly processed in the Reactor's mind.

The more controversial the image being created, the more time it will take for the Reactor to compare all previous sides of the issue, to decide whether to agree or disagree with your side. The more detailed or complex the image, the more time is needed for the Reactor to complete the picture being created and file it. Giving the Reactor enough time to process all of these images through the use of adequate pauses is an essential responsibility of the Presenter.

When you fail to pause, you fail to give a Reactor sufficient time to create images in her mind. When you pile on image after image without a break, she doesn't have time to go through the entire mental process for each image. She will soon be so far behind in your stream of images that she will have no choice but to disconnect from the conversation in search of images she *can* grasp. Often she will do so simply by retreating into her own mind, where she can enjoy her own images, that is, daydreaming.

Consider each individual image you create as a single brick, which, when placed next to other bricks, will soon become a row. Then you begin another row on top of that one, and another, until eventually, every row contributes to the completion of the wall, which is your entire presentation.

The mortar that holds those bricks together is the *pause*. The bigger the brick, the more mortar is needed to make it secure; in other words, the bigger the image, the longer the pause that is needed to in-sure that the image develops securely in the Reactor's mind.

Further, consider that each brick is one of those "thought bytes" discussed earlier. Each thought byte should create an image unto itself, which, when layered upon other images, will create the whole picture. Understanding that each thought byte needs to be an image by itself yet contributes toward one overall image will help you tremendously, whether you are having a one-on-one conversation, giving an extemporaneous presentation, or even writing a script.

The beauty of the pause is that in addition to allowing the Reactor to receive your previous image and correlate it to her own liking, it also provides you, the Presenter, with time to formulate your *next* thought byte! The pause is just as valuable to you, as Presenter, as it is necessary to the Reactor to file away her images.

The Length of the Pause

The length of a pause varies in accordance with the importance of the image it surrounds. The best way to determine the appropriate length of a pause to suit one's own purposes is to equate them to the importance of spaces between words on a written page. Without appropriate spaces, it would be nearly impossible for the "runtogetherlettersto-communicateeffectively," just as a conversation without pauses would have the same confusing and incomprehensible effect.

Obviously, the development of the written word is an extension of the way we talk, and came about as a way to satisfy the very specific human need to create individual images, just as we do when we speak. On the written page, one space between words is enough to indicate a distinction between words, yet a sentence requires a period at the end followed by two spaces to clearly separate it from the next thought. Paragraphs require an even further distinction, skipping to the next line and indenting, indicating a boundary between two even more distinct ideas.

In the same way, pauses are used to separate images. The more distinctly different the images are from one another, the longer the pause must be. Very long pauses are generally considered "pregnant," because they create a great moment of tremendous anticipation, the birth of something new that adds to the Reactor's previous knowledge. In the written word, this might be considered a cliffhanger chapter ending.

Shorter pauses would be like sentences and paragraphs, separating topics, emphasizing particular points, or simply giving you time to comfortably change your subject.

Again, in a one-on-one conversation, these pauses are automatic, part of our established norms. When we enter the world of presentation, however, pauses often go by the wayside, as we've previously noted. Fortunately, we can replicate many of our pauses by incorporating them into the system we have already begun to develop, by adding another layer of understanding to it.

Quite simply, the amount of time it takes for you to change your eye contact and full frontal stance from one focal point to another is conveniently just the right amount of time for all of your ordinary pauses to occur. During your turn, your Reactor will have time to proceed through the five steps she needs to in order to file away the previous image, and you will be able to formulate the next image in your brain at the same time.

Pauses while facing to your side focuses are like periods at the end of a sentence, allowing you to move from sentence to sentence with ease; pauses while looking to your center focus are like starting a new and important paragraph, requiring you take more time to delineate between this thought byte and the ones surrounding it.

Remember, we said the most important thought bytes should be reserved for those in the center focus, which means the pauses surrounding that center thought byte should be longer, both before and after—before, because it will create anticipation and attention for what you are about to say, and after, so the Reactor has time to fully assimilate that strong new image.

Should it take you longer to formulate your thoughts than it takes the Reactor to do her filing, all the better, as she will now sense that your pause indicates something even more important is about to be said, and will pay greater attention. If you simply use the method of turning to your focuses between each thought byte, the correct pause happens almost naturally.

The replication of natural pauses is one of the most valuable elements a Presenter can master. They provide the necessary time for the Reactor to create mental images, as well as provide you as the Presenter time to do the same. By simply incorporating the proper turning between focal points, you will pause in a perfectly natural way, will avoid pause fillers, and will meet the norms of the Reactor.

It is also quite natural for a Reactor to accept a longer than normal pause when the image being presented is more dramatic than normal. When you as a Presenter want to truly separate an image from all other images, simply extend the pause as long as you can stand it, then wait another few seconds. The longer the pause, the more dramatic the image will be. When it's a big brick, it needs lots of mortar!

Experiment with this fourth element of the **pause**, both in conversation and presentation. This is truly a fun element to use.

In addition to the value of a pause for the pause's sake, the pause is also an extraordinarily valuable tool for creating and maintaining an appropriate pace, which is our next element.

The Power of Pace

The basic rule of human nature is that powerful people
speak slowly and subservient people quickly—because if they
don't speak fast, nobody will listen to them.
—MICHAEL CAINE

Once you know how to make the most use out of your pauses, you must then determine how to make your best use out of the actual pace of the words you use in between the pauses.

During a one-on-one conversation, pace begins with the image. Imagine you are describing a beautiful piece of art. You would quite naturally match your pace to the part of the description to which it applied: perhaps slow around the curves, staccato around the falling leaves, or quickly with the pace of the speeding carriage, and so on. The uses and applications of pace are quite obvious when you are aware of their effects.

Similarly, once you have an image in your mind, you merely need to apply the pace, or more accurately, let the word center of your brain establish the proper pace for that image. In a normal conversation, you simply give yourself the freedom to use the appropriate pace as the image calls for it.

Pace comes into play most significantly, of course, when action words are employed. For example, when you want to impress upon your Reactor the speed at which something occurred, it is natural to speed up the pace of your words to promote a sense of urgency. You also naturally slow down your words to promote a sense of tardiness, tranquillity, laziness, or other similar characteristic or event.

When a Presenter uses a pace that is inconsistent with the content or image being presented, however, these incongruities between what the Presenter is saying and what he means will set off the intuitive alarm bells in the Reactor. Were a teacher to relate the story of the tortoise and the hare in reverse, describing the tortoise's actions quickly and the hare's slowly, the students would see it as an incongruity, even a lie, and they would lose trust in the teacher who seems to be selling them a bill of goods.

Simply by adjusting your pace to suit each individual image or thought byte, which will vary naturally as common sense would dictate, you can be assured of replicating one of the best elements of a one-on-one conversation.

The Pitfall of Plodding

One of the things that can go wrong with pace is a phenomenon known as "plodding." It occurs most often when someone is reading from a prepared text. Plodding is when the pace is exactly the same from beginning to end, unvarying and continuous. It is one of the most common—and worst—offenses against proper pacing. It causes the audience to lose interest, and to lose the essential thread of trust that ties them to the speaker.

Let's suppose the teacher in the earlier example was to treat the actions of both the tortoise and the hare equally, never changing the pace to match the image at all. That would be an example of plodding. Quite simply, plodding is the repetition of the same pace over and over again, regardless of the image being described. As we've said several times already, **repetition is the enemy of naturalness** and must be avoided.

Resist Racing

The other thing that most often goes wrong with pace is what is known as "racing."

First, remember that the opening moments of a presentation are critical. In many cases, this is the first time your Reactor will see and hear you, and, as the old saying goes, you only have one chance to make a first impression. You must know exactly what to do and why, so that you can make the most out of the opportunity.

Whenever anything new enters the scan of our senses, it takes a few moments for us to register, classify, compare, and judge it, before we can turn our attention back to the present moment. This means that the first words you utter, your pitch, your volume, whether you have a squeaky voice or a rich bass, whether the voice fits your body or the image you project, all must be scrutinized and judged before the Reactor will allow herself to relax and actually start to listen to what you are saying. This takes time, and as the Presenter, you are responsible for providing the Reactor that time.

Unfortunately, what usually happens at the beginning of a presentation is quite the opposite. Very often the Presenter, having been waiting for his turn to speak, has so much pent-up energy that the moment he reaches the lectern or platform, he begins his presentation like a racehorse bursting out of the starting gate!

He will then continue to gallop along until he either settles down, which could take seconds to minutes depending on his own comfort level, or until he reaches the end of his message, whichever comes first. In some cases, he never settles down regardless of the length of the race, continuing to speak as fast as possible, since the sooner he gets to the end of his message, the sooner this whole thing will be over!

Obviously, if you as the Presenter deliver such a speedy opening, the Reactor will not have the time she needs to analyze your voice in any way, shape, or form. By the time she finally does reach a comfort level with it, you will be so far into your message that she will have gleaned none of the images you have presented, and she will have to work very hard to get caught up. She will only do so if your message is sufficiently compelling. If your pace continues to be too fast throughout, she won't bother.

Take note that even when a Reactor has heard your voice before in other situations, she must be given sufficient time to hear it again in this situation for the same assimilation to occur. The acoustics of the room may make the voice sound different, the number of people may have an effect, and so on. Regardless of the previous history with the Reactor, *you must give your Reactor time to become accustomed to your voice each time you begin a presentation.*

Get Off to a Slow Start

This can best be accomplished simply by deliberately starting off slowly. This may be more difficult than it sounds, because when a Presenter has pent-up energy, it takes discipline to control it. Interestingly, though, a Presenter's sense of "slowness," when attached to nervous energy, will actually come out sounding just about like a normal pace, which in most cases is just fine. You must take care to deliberately begin more slowly than what may seem natural in order to replicate what, in fact, would actually be the norm.

Sometimes it is necessary to go even more slowly, such as when the room or the crowd is very large, or when there is a lot of ambient noise, just to give the Reactor more time to adjust to the sound of the Presenter's voice. The only caveat is that it shouldn't be so artificially deliberately slow as to register as false or ridiculous.

These moments should be considered as a kind of "settling in" of your voice, just like settling into a comfortable old armchair. It takes a minute to get all the right parts of the body in all of the right places, just as it takes a Reactor to settle in and get comfortable with your voice. Usually, the amount of time necessary for the Reactor to get settled in is pretty much the same amount of time it takes for the Presenter to get settled in. Once this settling has occurred, it requires little further thought or consideration, and the pace applied to your images will be correct.

Should you have an accent different from much of your audience, however, you may have to slow down for a bit longer. It takes a few extra minutes of adjustment for the Reactor to identify an accent than it does to merely register the type of voice you have. As such, it requires a slightly slower pace or longer introduction period to get the Reactor appropriately accustomed to that difference.

Contrary to popular belief, a Presenter with an accent has a distinct advantage over those Presenters with a more common speech pattern. For most Reactors, it is more interesting to listen to, and even though it may seem to take a bit more effort, a Reactor actually pays *more* attention to the words and message of a Presenter with an accent than she might with a more familiar vocal pattern.

In addition, the Reactor, recognizing the existence of a norm different from her own, will be compelled to consider what is said more carefully to avoid misunderstanding at all levels of the conversation. Therefore, when properly paced, a Presenter with an accent, whether regional or international, can actually encourage greater listening.

So while the pace of your presentation will mostly be determined by the images as they pass through the word center of your brain, you must be aware enough to avoid plodding and racing. Remember that the beginning of your presentation must be slowed down deliberately in order to ensure the Reactor has time to become accustomed to your voice.

The Versatility of Volume

I want to see you shoot the way you shout.
—THEODORE ROOSEVELT

Volume is another element ruled by the Goldilocks principle of too much, too little, and just right. Further, the principle can be applied to two different aspects of volume: the **actual** volume, and the **variety** of volume.

First, let's look at the norms of actual volume. We know quite intimately from our own norms when it is appropriate to be loud and when it is appropriate to be soft, when a whisper is more suitable than a shout. The origin of volume originates from two norms: the image and the situation.

First, the image we have in mind will suggest what kind of volume is necessary, be it a shout, a whisper, or a simple conversational tone. During a normal one-on-one encounter, common sense easily dictates what volume to use for that image, providing the situation allows it.

The situation can secondarily change our volume. Perhaps we are very excited about something, and our word center is telling us to speak loudly to show our excitement, but there is a sleeping baby in the next room. We know we must lower the volume for the situation, overriding the volume dictated by the image. This is all part of our established norms and requires little additional thought.

When the situation moves into a presentational one, however, the use of volume can often become problematic.

Usually the problem is too much volume. When a Presenter is faced with a very large room, the compulsion will often be to speak louder, to insure that he will be heard in the back row. Unfortunately, too much volume, particularly for an extended period of time, sounds like shouting.

This happens more often than it should. For some reason, many Presenters get into "speech mode," regardless of the venue or the electronic assistance available. They feel it is necessary to project as loudly as the old-time politician on the back of a hay wagon. In all but the rarest of instances, that type of speech making is long gone, and should be duly buried.

This is particularly true when a speech is being televised. Imagine the poor Reactor at home trying to watch, but the Presenter is yelling at the top of his lungs, perhaps because the Presenter is in a large room somewhere and he thinks he has to yell to be heard in the last row.

To those watching at home, the Presenter comes across like one of those pitchmen selling stain remover as loud as he can. What do we normally do when someone starts yelling at us on TV? We change the channel as soon as possible. It's the same when someone is standing in our living room. Were they to start yelling at us, we'd likely ask them to leave. No one wants to get yelled at, especially in their own home, yet that's exactly what happens when a speaker goes into high-volume "speech mode."

The other end of the spectrum is too little volume. If you speak with too little volume, the Reactor can't hear you, unless you have electronic assistance such as a microphone. Even then it is possible to be too quiet to be heard. Obviously, you must have enough volume to be heard, so you must either speak louder or better yet, have the microphone turned up.

The idea is to speak in accordance with the image and not to be thrown by the situation. Very often when a conversation becomes a presentation, the tendency is to overcompensate with volume, and you must resist the urge. Your volume should be dictated more by the image than the situation, as your response to the situation (for example, a large room) may be counterproductive. You must strive to replicate the actual volume that your image dictates would occur in a one-on-one situation, so that you always sound conversational, rather than "speechy."

The other factor that involves volume has to do with the **variety** of volume used.

During a normal conversation, volume varies in accordance with each image. The same must occur in every other venue to insure you meet the norms of a conversation.

When it comes to variety, too little variety in your volume would become repetitious. A single volume, regardless of whether it is all soft, all loud, or somewhere in the middle, becomes repetitious, and, as you know by now, **repetition is the enemy of naturalness.**

Too much variety of volume is something that occurs so rarely that it hardly needs mentioning, though you should be aware that it is possible. When someone changes volume to the degree that it sounds artificial, it will send the Reactor's intuitive alarm bells ringing.

Ultimately, the most important consideration of the element of volume in conversation is that volume must remain variable, just as it does during normal, natural conversation, and must be appropriate to the image being presented, as determined during the creation of your image.

Once the image is set, you merely need to apply the volume, or more accurately, let the word center of your brain establish the proper volume for that image. Then give yourself the freedom to use that appropriate volume and volume variety.

Acoustics 101

In addition to sensibly matching the volume and volume variety to each image, you should be aware of a few other technical considerations. First are the size and acoustics of the room, particularly in cases where there will be no electronic amplification of the presentation.

Naturally, the larger the room, the more volume will be necessary to reach the back row. The same is true for rooms with higher ceilings. The more fabric in the room, like curtains, wall hangings, flocked wallpaper, and carpets, the more sound will be absorbed; thus, the more volume will be necessary to overcome that absorption.

Rooms with less fabric and more hard surfaces, like linoleum floors, paneled walls, and plaster ceilings, present the opposite acoustic problems, namely that sound bounces off of them. In such a case, volume can usually be reduced, as the hard surfaces allow sound to travel more quickly, though actually, volume plays second fiddle to pace on these occasions. The more hard surfaces, the slower your pace should be, and the longer your pauses.

That's because since the words are bouncing backward and forward, you must give each thought byte time to stop reverberating and settle down before you begin the next thought byte. Generally speaking, this will make the presentation move more slowly, so when time is a consideration, such acoustical limitations must be taken into account when determining the length of the script.

Of course, the acoustics of every room will change in accordance with the number of people and, to a lesser degree, the amount of clothing they are wearing or carrying. Again, each audience member represents a certain amount of absorption of sound, and an astute Presenter should note the differences. For a true audiophile, even the types of chairs will make a substantial difference, since metal folding chairs will bounce more sound than padded ones.

Naturally, the great outdoors is the biggest room of all, with the most absorption possible in any environment, out into the atmosphere. Though such a presentation would have to be projected more loudly than most others, you must still take care to use variety and avoid staying at the same loud volume constantly, lest the enemy—repetition—set in. When you have technical assistance, such as a microphone or other amplification system, you must be careful to remember that you no longer need concern yourself with increasing your volume to fill the room, as the amplification system will now accomplish this. The moment you realize there is a working microphone in the room, your only consideration regarding volume should be its appropriateness to the images in your presentation.

The Paintbrush of Pitch

Speech is an arrangement of notes that will never
be played again.
—F. SCOTT FITZGERALD

Pitch simply refers to the limitless variations inherent in every human's vocal capacity, in the same way that "range" describes the capacity of a singer or a musical instrument. Every one of us has a range of pitches that we are capable of using, and we use them for a variety of reasons.

The best way to understand this concept is to imagine your vocal pitch as being on a scale from 0 to 10, with 0 being the most dynamic expression of the lower range (bass) of the voice, and 10 being the most dynamic expression of the higher range (soprano) of the voice.

During ordinary, one-on-one conversations about typical, everyday subjects, the amount of variation we use in the pitch of our voices will generally range from around 3 to 7, using all points in between to effectively express our images, as seen in Figure 4.

As we become more excited, intense, or passionate, our range

Figure 4. Ordinary Vocal Pitch Range

will vary considerably more, as much as from 1 to 10—as seen in Figure 5—in order to provide more color to the image we are describing. At times of the most extreme need, such as to voice a warning about impending physical danger like an oncoming car, we use

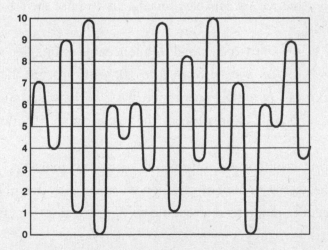

Figure 5. Extreme Emergency Range

our most intense pitch to create the necessary sense of urgency as the situation calls for it.

Whenever a Presenter uses a smaller range of pitch than what he would use in normal conversation—in essence, using the same few pitches over and over—he inevitably creates repetition of those pitches, and (all together now!) **repetition is the enemy of naturalness.**

The worst (or rather, best) example of repetition in pitch comes in the form of the monotone (Figure 6), where the pitch remains the same or in a very limited range, throughout the presentation. Few things will cause a Reactor to lose interest faster than a message delivered in a monotone.

If a Presenter uses a wider range of pitch than what would ordinarily be called for given the situation, he will come across as going over the top, and will, once again, set off a Reactor's intuitive alarm bells.

Ordinarily in a normal conversation, or whenever we are giving a

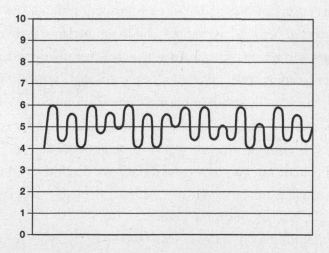

Figure 6. Monotone

spontaneous presentation, pitch is correctly established by the image. Once you have determined your image, you merely need to let the word center of your brain establish the proper pitch for that image. Then, as with so many other elements of conversation, you must give yourself the freedom to use that appropriate pitch.

There is one extremely prevalent exception, however, that occurs whenever we begin to read, as in the case with scripted or highly prepared presentations.

Using Pitch with a Script

In all but the very rarest cases, the moment most Presenters begin to read aloud, the natural, normal 3 to 7 range of vocal variety shrinks dramatically. It suddenly and inexplicably becomes reduced to a 4 to 6 range (Figure 7), or worse, the dreaded 5 monotone, guaranteeing even the most avid Reactor will fall asleep or zone out.

This occurs primarily due to early reading training. As each of us learns to read out loud during our childhood, we mistakenly learn that there is a certain, narrow cadence that is generally considered an acceptable "reading style," though it bears strikingly little resemblance to the way we actually speak in normal conversation.

The pattern of this ingrained reading cadence requires that we start the beginning of each sentence at about 6 on our scale, and gradually slide our way downward until we reach the end of the sentence, winding up on about a 4 (think, "I pledge allegiance to the flag . . ."). No risk of drama here.

While this may be an easy way to keep everyone in the class reading the same way, and perhaps allow a teacher to more easily spot a

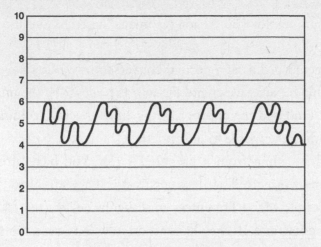

Figure 7. Reading Cadence

student having problems, in the long run, it establishes a monotonous reading cadence that many people find almost impossible to break, even in adulthood. That's assuming we even want to break the habit. Imagine if everyone saying the Pledge of Allegiance or the Lord's Prayer all used their own personal inflections and pitch? It would no doubt sound somewhat chaotic.

Unfortunately, once established, these habits are extremely hard to break, even when we are older and know better. We are indoctrinated to believe that reading should sound like reading. To make more out of the words on the page than dictated from childhood makes us feel uncomfortable, even guilty. We end up being self-conscious readers, unaware or unable to incorporate a more realistic, conversational vocal pitch into our reading.

In order to overcome this challenge, we can either deliberately adjust our pitch purposefully, as a skilled and classically trained actor or radio personality would do through years of schooling and experience, or we can employ the "Thought-Image" process we use in natural conversation.

Remember, during a normal conversation we first have a thought in our mind. Next, we create the words to describe the image of that thought (and add the appropriate gestures, pacing, volume, etc.) before sending the words to our mouth.

When reading from a prepared script, you have already determined the words to describe your image. They are already set down in the script. Many Presenters mistakenly believe that the "image" work is done, and all they have to do now is to read the words, and the Reactor will be able to get the image from that. They shortcut everything that goes to the brain except the connection between the eyes that read the words and the mouth that speaks them. Yet as we've said before, **words alone are never enough!**

By skipping past the image-creation portion of the mental process, you will inevitably omit the "pitch-creation" process as well (not to mention the gesture, pacing, and volume center, among others!). The result is that because no image has actually been created (or re-created) in your mind, no accompanying pitch can be applied to it either. This will result in monotone or near monotone.

To reincorporate the image-creation process of our brains, we must see the written words, return those words to the image center of the brain in order to re-create that image, and finally, describe that image with the words we've already selected and written. By *describing* the image rather than merely spewing forth words, you set in motion the proper chronology of physical and verbal elements, which will create the essential norms.

While this might seem like an impossible task, it is, in fact, a feat accomplished by every person who has learned to break the mold of the reading cadence. The best example is an actor who must first read the script, create the image of what those words mean in his own mind, learn those images, then redescribe that image when the time comes, using the words already written for him by the playwright or screenwriter. It's another element that simply takes practice and experience.

Fortunately, the time that it takes for you to formulate the image in your own mind is the exact same time you're giving to the Reactor for absorbing the previous image, that *pause* between each image as discussed earlier. In essence, the very same pause the Reactor uses to understand your last image is the same pause you use to create your next image.

The pause is your thinking time, your *image*-making time. When the words originate from the image, rather than the words, your mind will automatically reincorporate all of the normal elements of conversation. The larger the image, the more time it takes to recreate it in your mind, the longer the pause, and the more anticipation will be built in the Reactor.

When you are using a written or memorized script, this process is one of the most critical for you to fully understand and master in order to eliminate the deeply entrenched habit of the reading cadence. When you sound like you are reading, you have not captured the essence of a one-on-one conversation, and your presentation will be less successful.

That is why it is so important to clearly understand and master our seventh element of **pitch.**

It should be clear by now that much of the naturalness in a presentation comes from understanding that there is an image behind the words, and that when the Presenter has a clear idea of the image he wishes to convey, the brain is very good at adding all of the physical and verbal elements that are appropriate to that image: gestures, pauses, pacing, volume, and pitch. These elements are all added after the image is created in the Presenter's mind, either spontaneously or through the re-creation of words on a page.

Now that we know what physical and vocal elements must be added to the words, it's time to become more familiar with the tools of the trade, beginning with one of the biggest debates in the presentational arena: whether or not to use a written script.

PART 4

The Tools of the Trade

Seven Essential Tools for Your Presentation Toolbox

There are dozens of actual tools of the trade that can be employed by a Presenter. The following are the most common and basic, and therefore the ones you will most likely encounter. Any time you are faced with a new tool, however, simply determine what element of a conversation that tool is supposed to enhance, observe how that element occurs in a normal one-on-one conversation, and strive to figure out a way to replicate that outcome. If all else fails, call or e-mail us for an answer!

Your Script

Speak clearly if you speak at all; carve every word
before you let it fall.
—OLIVER WENDELL HOLMES

In the often heated debate over whether to use a script or to simply "wing it," there are pros and cons for both sides of the issue. Some Presenters see the script as a necessity to insure they remember everything and remain organized, on track, or politically correct. Others see it as a straitjacket (which, when used improperly, it can be). They understand that appearing natural is the key, and believe they can only capture that naturalness by delivering extemporaneously, with or without notes. Very often, the event will dictate whether a script is necessary or if an extemporaneous presentation will do. Whichever the case, a seasoned Presenter should know how to do both.

Before we begin discussing the right way to prepare a script or notes, however, there are a few common myths that first need to be dispelled, lest we fall prey to the many rampant old wives' tales about scripts.

Because we know that looking natural is a major key for successful presenting, we recognize the reality that when an audience sees us reading a script it detracts from that naturalness. Many Presenters have historically responded to that problem by making the physical size of the script smaller in the hope the audience won't notice. Thus the immortalization of one of the worst script ideas of all time: writing speeches on index cards.

First of all, index cards are just plain ugly, and, contrary to their purpose (of being small and therefore harder to see), almost every Reactor will see them every time a new card is flipped over, which, because the cards are so small, seems to be about every ten seconds or so. Each time a card is flipped, it reminds the Reactor that the Presenter is reading. Every time the Reactor is reminded the Presenter is reading, she is further reminded that the Presenter doesn't seem to know what he is talking about, thus diminishing his credibility.

Second, it looks unprofessional, like kids getting ready to trade bubble gum baseball cards or students preparing for a book report. It can't help but come across as amateurish.

Third, consider the consequences of the cards getting mixed up, falling on the floor, or accidentally rotating upside down and sideways from being inside your pocket. Fiddling with such cards for even a moment will create the impression of disorganization, unprofessionalism, and lack of confidence and knowledge on the subject at hand. When a Presenter appears less organized than his Reactor, there is little hope that the presentation will be well received.

Just as bad is a script written on a legal or writing pad. First of all, it is just plain ugly. Second, when the pages are detached, there is still the risk of getting them mixed up and out of order. Third, handwriting is infinitely harder to read than typing; therefore, making errors in the message is much more likely. When the purpose of a script is to get the message right, this is a sorry and ineffective way to go.

Fourth, when the pages are left attached, it requires the Presenter to pick up the pad, turn the first page over the top, and set the pad back down again. Each time the Presenter does so, he reminds the Reactor that he is, indeed, reading. So much for being surreptitious in your use of a script!

Since the Presenter's purpose when using a script is to be more organized and exacting in his message, it is necessary for that impression to be carried throughout the presentation. The best way to accomplish this with a fully prepared script, or even when you are just using notes or an outline for an extemporaneous presentation, is to carry the script in a ring-type binder, preferably the thin, one-inch type. We recommend a very nice leather binder, perhaps bearing a company or organizational logo in order to look even more professional.

By using a professional-looking folder, you as the Presenter will appear as though you are "coming to work," that you are fully organized, and you will exude determination, confidence, and authority. Such an image will come across as very "take charge," which is precisely what a Reactor wants to see from a Presenter.

It indicates that you have important things to say, thus assuring the Reactor she isn't wasting her time, that you will provide her with new and credible information, rather than anything you're making up off the top of your head. Even if the you almost never refer to the notebook, the fact that you walked up there with it sets the tone for the entire event.

Having been printed in large type (sixteen- to twenty-point, depending on your eyesight), the script should be placed in the binder in such a way that when the binder is open, two full pages of script appear before you, one scripted page on each side. Page 1 will be on the left side, page 2 on the right. When you turn a page, page 3 will be on the left, 4 on the right, and so on.

This can be accomplished by either placing the pages inside a plastic cover with a page on each side (be careful with this, as overhead lights can often create glare on some plastic sheets that will make it difficult to read—look for the slightly textured sheets), or by printing, gluing, stapling, or otherwise attaching two pages together back to back.

While it's true that every time you turn a page you do momentarily remind the Reactor that you are reading from a script, by having two pages open at once, you will turn pages half as often, thus diminishing the distraction as much as possible.

When it does come time to turn the page, you should turn the page as you are moving your body toward your new focal point. This means it is necessary that a thought byte should always be complete on a given page, rather than split between pages. The Reactor will be busy watching your whole body move, either toward her or toward someone else, as well as filing away the last image you just presented, so she will scarcely notice the simple hand flick you will be giving the next page of your script.

Remember that when you turn to your new focus, you are providing time for your Reactor to digest and file the previous image away, plus giving yourself time to be thinking about the image of your next thought byte as you turn to your new focus. It forces you to incorporate a wonderful and essential pause between each thought byte, which is just as it should be.

When a script is fully prepared, using it will require almost no thinking on your part, which is exactly what you want. Even in the best of circumstances, you will have far too many unexpected, uncontrollable things to distract you without having to be concerned about those things that can and should be expected and controlled through proper preparation.

Now that we know how a script should look when it's done, it's time to determine exactly what needs to be in it.

Script Layout for a Fully Prepared Script

As discussed previously, every script is made up of thought bytes approximately twenty-five to forty words long. Each thought byte should encompass one complete image, and its length delineates when and how long a Presenter should remain at one focal point.

Remember that the creation of these paragraphs has no resemblance to the written paragraph as the rules normally apply, as seen in the example of the Gettysburg Address. These paragraphs simply telegraph to you an impossible-to-ignore reminder of when it is time to change your focal point. One thought-bite paragraph equals one focal point, pure and simple.

In addition to being an obvious physical reminder for changing focus and all that goes along with it, the thought-bite paragraphs serve many other useful purposes for assisting you in the preparation and writing of your script.

The first advantage of these paragraphs is to insure that the speech is, indeed, written as a speech, rather than merely the regurgitation of a report, the reading of an essay, or the presentation of information. It is truly surprising how many Presenters think that a speech is little more than the simple transmission of information. It must be absolutely clear that without at least some inspiration, information is useless.

Writing a speech is substantially different than writing almost any other type of communication. Obvious as this may seem (though often ignored nonetheless), speeches must be written with the thought of them being spoken aloud in mind. By writing in thought bytes, you can easily spot overly long sentences and images that are unclear from the way they are written, and you can determine whether each thought byte sounds conversational.

As you begin to put your thoughts on paper in the thought-bite paragraphs, you will soon discover that a consistent pattern will emerge, one that will actually assist you in deciding how a series of thoughts should flow, and even which thought byte will be said to which focus.

As mentioned earlier, the first thought byte, the last thought byte, and the thought bytes expressing the strongest points should be made to the center focus. The remaining thought bytes need to be split between each side.

We know that the opening phrase must be addressed to the center focus, and it must be one that will identify with your Reactor, a statement with which your Reactor can agree. (Four score and seven years ago, our fathers brought forth on this continent a new nation . . .) Once you have made that opening statement of agreement to your front focus, you will turn to one of your side focuses to begin introducing new ideas. (Now we are engaged in a great civil war . . .)

As you progress though the description of your new idea, you will spread it evenly between both sides, until you reach a point strong enough to be directed at the center focus again. Depending on the extent of the new idea, that center focus could be either (1) the proposal of the action regarding that idea, in which case the identifier for your next new idea would be delivered to your next side focus, or (2) simply an emphatic point that needs to be made before continuing with that same idea, which will continue to subsequently be split between the side focuses. (The world will little note nor long remember what we say here, but it can never forget what they did here.)

A script with a good tempo built into it will generally express a good point worthy of being directed to the center approximately every five to seven thought bytes. This means that you can go from one side focus to another side focus two or three complete cycles before returning to the center focus with your next strong point.

Ordinarily, one or two cycles is enough to fully describe the new idea, or at least that layer of the idea, before it is time to begin a new cycle with a new idea.

By knowing that you must come back to the center focus at least every five to seven paragraphs, and that you must make a significant point when you do, you can insure your presentation will be evenly divided, that the sides will get the bulk of the speech, and the center will always get the strongest points.

It will also ensure that each new idea you are discussing gets the right amount of attention. *The more important the issue, the more cycles.*

Practice, Practice, Practice

Of course, the best way to see how that pattern emerges is to practice reading the script out loud. When a written script is used, it is essential that you spend time doing this. While this may seem obvious to many, a shocking number of Presenters write a script in the same way they write a report or letter, or worse, have a script written for them, and never actually read it aloud prior to the event. Suffice it to say that only a true neophyte thinks he can go out on a golf course and sink a hole in one. A professional knows that the more natural something appears, the more time went into making it appear that way.

First, reading the script out loud will assist you in becoming comfortable with the length of each thought byte, thus making it easier to become aware of your own natural time clock, as mentioned earlier. It will be easy to know when a thought byte is too short or too long.

Second, you will be able to detect any potential word or word combination difficulties. Should you experience any repeated discomfort, such as thought bytes that are too long or word groups that seem to cause your tongue to trip, you should reconsider the wording to make it more likely you can get through it. A Presenter who stumbles over the same place several times while practicing would be foolish to think it will come out right later, when the pressure of the occasion will inevitably make it more difficult. Better to reword it beforehand.

Third, reading a script aloud will give you the opportunity to get used to the opening and closing phrases that have been highlighted in each thought byte, so that you may remain in strong eye contact and full frontal contact with each focal point longer, as your need to look down at the middle of the sentence is reduced. This will allow you more freedom rather than being chained to every word of the script.

In addition to writing in thought bytes, highlighting the opening and closing phrases of each thought byte, and enlarging the size of the font in your script so that it is easier to read, you may also use additional symbols to remind yourself of other valuable information. For example, you can indicate when a particular paragraph should be said to the center or side focuses, even to **which** side focus. This can be done simply by the insertion of a few easy-to-remember symbols at the end of each thought byte paragraph. For example:

Indicates turn to center focus
* Indicates turn to side focus
> Indicates turn to right focus or < turn to left focus
// Indicates break or extra long pause between phrases

To see how all of these elements are used, here is the beginning of the Gettysburg Address again, to demonstrate these tools:

FOUR SCORE AND SEVEN YEARS AGO, OUR FATHERS **brought forth on this continent a new nation, conceived in liberty, and dedicated to the proposition** THAT ALL MEN ARE CREATED EQUAL. * >

NOW WE ARE ENGAGED IN A GREAT CIVIL WAR, **testing whether that nation, or any nation so conceived and so dedicated, can long endure. We are** MET ON A GREAT BATTLEFIELD OF THAT WAR. * <

WE HAVE COME TO DEDICATE A PORTION OF THAT FIELD as a final resting-place for those who here gave their lives that that nation might live. // It is altogether FITTING AND PROPER WE SHOULD DO THIS. * >

BUT IN A LARGER SENSE, WE CANNOT DEDICATE, we cannot consecrate, we cannot hallow this ground. The brave men, living and dead, who struggled here have consecrated it FAR ABOVE OUR POOR POWER TO ADD OR DETRACT. ##

THE WORLD WILL LITTLE NOTE NOR LONG REMEMBER what we say here. But it can NEVER FORGET WHAT THEY DID HERE. * >

Note how the symbol for what to do next is at the *end* of the previous thought byte, except the opening paragraph. This will insure that you will see it early enough to know where you are going on the next thought byte, before it is too late!

By preparing a script in this manner, you provide yourself with a security blanket that will cover just about everything that could possibly go wrong. You are completely organized, so there is no chance of forgetting anything, and you have every moment of your presentation accounted for. The only thing left to do is to practice it enough to make it appear natural.

The great thing about this system is that even though the first few times you practice will feel very uncomfortable, stilted, and programmed, when you keep practicing, it will soon become second nature, and every script you use hereafter will get easier and easier.

It's just like learning a new tennis or golf swing. The first few times (or few dozen times!), it will feel stiff and look unnatural. After a while, the body memory takes over, and you'll no longer have to think about it. It will all appear to happen naturally.

The same thing will happen with using this method of scripting. Eventually it will become so second nature that writing a script will be incredibly easy because it will be all thought bytes, and performing the script will be easy because every possible contingency has been taken into consideration, and you will be fully protected by your security blanket!

So instead of being the straitjacket so many Presenters fear, your script becomes a valuable security blanket for those occasions when your message must be exact, such as at major corporate or stockholders' meetings, political events, conventions, public hearings, or any other situation that requires every word be perfectly accurate.

For less critical occasions, for events that are more casual, or for material with which you are already comfortable, you can simply write an outline, such as the one on page 54, using the Formula for Inspiration to delineate your opening statement, your topics, and your closing statement. Even when simply using an outline, however, you will enhance your professional appearance when you put it in that leather binder we described earlier.

So when you are invited to make a presentation, you must first decide "to script, or not to script," based on the occasion, the venue, and the importance of getting every word correct. Whether you choose to use a script or an outline, you now have the tools in your toolbox to do both.

Your Mantle of Authority

You're only as good as your last performance.
—THEATRICAL SAGE

All the world's a stage . . .
—WILLIAM SHAKESPEARE

Seldom have truer words ever been spoken than those in the above observation from Shakespeare.

Every one of us is obliged to adopt certain behaviors that are indicated by the position we occupy. Each of us can behave both as an adult and a child, an intimate and a stranger, a boss and an employee, depending on the situation at hand.

So, too, must a Presenter accept the responsibility of the role that goes along with making a presentation: the role of authority. Authority, in this case, means simply that you, as Presenter, appear to have a greater understanding or knowledge regarding the subject of discussion at this moment in time than your Reactor. A litany of titles and credentials are not necessary to establish authority, only that you have more knowledge on a certain subject than your Reactor. After all, a security guard or limousine chaffeur knows more about some subjects than a corporate CEO.

Ben Bradley of the *Washington Post* once said that he wouldn't have cared if Deep Throat, the informant in the Watergate Scandal of the early 1970s, had been a janitor. It mattered only that the information he was providing was correct, and was more than anyone else publicly knew at the time.

Whether it is a low-level floor manager making a presentation to the board of directors or a duly elected president addressing a nation, that Presenter must represent authority, must be *the leader for that moment in time.*

Regardless of what your position may actually be in comparison to your Reactors, whenever you stand before a group, you must accept the mantle of responsibility for being the leader, for as long as you are before that group.

Reactors expect certain behavior from a leader. They expect a certain carriage, a certain style, a certain attire, a certain "way of going." When a Presenter first appears before them, Reactors will invariably give that Presenter the benefit of the doubt that he has the authority to stand before them. When a Presenter fails to take that benefit of the doubt and confirm that judgment relatively quickly, the Reactors will inevitably be disappointed. That is the norm.

Understanding that it is necessary to accept that mantle of authority is only the first step toward actually wearing it. Successfully wearing it is actually accomplished less often than you would think. We all know leaders, and in particular a certain president of the United States, who do not appear to accept their mantle of authority, who fail to exhibit the kind of behavior we Reactors expect from a person in that position. The result is our disappointment because our expectation of a leader, our norms for that leader, are not met. This inevitably undermines the Alliance we wish to have with him (and that he should want from us), making him less of a leader than he could and should be. It's imperative a leader behave like one!

So when you begin to prepare for an actual event, in addition to the imagery you must create within your message, you must also take on the personal image of the authority, the expert, and ultimately, the leader, in order to satisfy the needs of the Reactor you will shortly be facing. This requires not only accepting the mantle of authority, but also actually wearing it. For that, we need to incorporate a number of additional elements, all of which will assist you in becoming the leader your Reactor demands.

Your Attire

Clothes make the man (or woman).
—ANONYMOUS

It is an interesting question how far man would retain their
relative rank if they were divested of their clothes.
—HENRY DAVID THOREAU

The first thing anyone usually notices about someone is their attire. Instant judgments are attached to certain types of clothing. We recognize a homeless person because of the way he dresses; we know a parochial school student because of the uniform; we know a soldier, a CEO, and a movie star all by the clothes they wear.

While much time and energy has been devoted toward figuring out the psychological effects of color, patterns, styles, and countless other factors, for the most part, few Reactors ever really take notice of such particulars. The only judgment they usually make is whether or not they agree with that person's particular taste, or whether the attire warrants a higher level of respect (for example, in the case of a particular uniform, the reaction to which is entirely subjective and impossible to predict).

As Presenter, you must be aware of attire inasmuch as it must promote a leadership image. This actually has more to do with how your attire compares to that of your Reactor, than the attire you decide to wear yourself. It has to do with how your clothing will make the Reactor feel toward you. There are some very easy guidelines that can help you determine the Reactor's response, and a simple way to control them.

Go "One Step Up"

Since we know that in the opening of a presentation you must do all you can to identify with your Reactor, and that your attire will probably be the first thing your Reactor notices, you must determine the expected attire of the Reactor at the occasion, then dress relative to that expectation, with one important variation. In order to establish on sight that you are the authority, you must dress *slightly better* than the Reactor, so that your attire supports the image that you have been successful as the result of your endeavors. Therefore, the most helpful rule of thumb is for you to dress "one-step-up" from your Reactors.

For example, for men, when the attire of the Reactor is jeans and a T-shirt, you should wear something like casual slacks and a collared pullover shirt. When the Reactor will be wearing casual slacks and a dress shirt, you should wear something like dress pants and a sports jacket. When the Reactor is in suit and tie, you should be in a better suit, perhaps vested and with a beautiful silk tie. For women, the strategy is the same. When your Reactor is in jeans, you should wear dress pants or a casual dress. When your Reactor is in dress pants, you should be wearing a nice suit or a more tailored dress, and so on.

Always dress "one step up" and your authority will be supported by your attire. Simply stated, you want your clothes to say, "I'm just like you, I just have a little more knowledge or authority. Therefore, I've been a little more successful on this particular subject."

Occasionally, you may be spontaneously called upon to speak before a group when your attire is unsuitable. Let's say you've just conducted a manager's meeting and are dressed in your business suit, and someone asks you to go to the plant floor and speak directly to the workers, who are in jeans or other casual wear. The simple answer is to loosen your tie, remove your jacket, even roll up your sleeves to adapt to the proper, one-step-up level.

When a Presenter goes overboard by dressing *far above* the Reactor, such as a three-piece suit to the Reactor's jeans and T-shirt, the Reactor will feel intimidated and will be ill-at-ease with the Presenter. The Reactor may begin to assume that the Presenter is making judgments against her, or is there to tell her how to do her own job or to "show off" the differences between them. It immediately creates a negativity that is very difficult to overcome.

Dressing *below* the Reactor is equally detrimental from a psychological point of view. When you fail to project an image of authority, it will be nearly impossible for you to be perceived as a leader. The Reactor will inevitably wonder, "Why should I listen to someone who dresses worse than I do?" or more specifically, "All his ideas haven't made *him* better off, so why should I listen?"

Dressing *at the same level* as the Reactor wrongly tells the Reactor that you are so much like her that she shouldn't expect you to have anything new to offer her, that you are equals on all levels. When you appear to be exactly the same as the Reactor, you will have difficulty establishing your authority, and your leadership won't be taken seriously.

While this may sound contradictory to the original premise that the first thing you say must identify with the Reactor, it is, in fact, exactly on point. Even though what you say in your opening indicates you and the Reactor are the same, your attire should indicate that there are some differences. When you begin to introduce your new ideas, those differences will become clear, and the Reactor will interpret your success (as indicated by your "better" attire) as an indication that you have capitalized on your ideas, and that she can, too.

In other words, you want to dress with the end goal in mind, rather than the beginning. Since the goal is to inspire the Reactor to join your successful Alliance, you want her to see what she can gain by doing so. Your attire will be an indicator of the success of that Alliance. Were you to wear the same level of clothes, there would be no indication that your knowledge has gained you anything, so it would be harder for the Reactor to believe that it will provide her any benefit.

Fashion Tips for TV

There are several technical elements you should know about clothing, particularly when an event is to be recorded for broadcast or posterity. Clothing with a very tight pattern, like a herringbone tie or closely striped shirt or dress, will cause most cameras to "shimmer" in an eye-catching and distracting way. When the eye is looking at shimmery clothing, there's little chance that the Reactor is hearing what is being said.

When you wear white, especially under bright lights, the camera will experience a little "flare," which will exaggerate the white and wash out an area larger than the white itself. For example, when a man wears a white shirt, it will flare around his face, and his face will appear much more washed out than it is.

To avoid that, wear a light blue shirt. Light blue will actually look almost white under the scrutiny of bright lights and a camera, but will prevent the possibility of flaring. The same thing should be considered for white suits, dresses, blouses, and so on.

Your Attire, Your Image

As helpful as attire is to creating an image of leadership, it is not, by itself, enough to give you the appearance of having accepted the mantle of authority. After all, were you to see someone in a $3,000 suit passed out on a bar, you wouldn't automatically assume he is a leader just because he's well dressed. Your behavior while you are dressed in your one-step-up attire is just as important as your attire itself.

Let's assume for the moment that you are an ambitious person, that you intend to advance in your chosen career. Consider what position you wish to hold in that field five or ten years from now. Do you suppose you would behave the same way in that position as you do now? Or would you stand up straighter, walk with more purpose, be more definitive in your actions, have more confidence in your ability to do the job?

It's a strange and wonderful thing, our human brain. Whenever we imagine something about ourselves, our bodies respond to that image. When we are feeling sexy and attractive, our walk and our stance change, and we outwardly exhibit all of the signs of being available. When we are feeling sad or depressed, our shoulders slump, our head drops, our facial expressions sink. Whatever image we have of ourselves, of how we feel at that moment, our bodies respond to that image.

Therefore, when you need to accept the mantle of authority in a presentational situation, you must imagine yourself as that leader, that accomplished and confident person that you intend to be five or ten years from now. Once that image is firmly established in your brain, your body will do the rest.

This little technique is where "stage presence" originates. Despite the common misconception that people with "presence" are born that way, it is, in fact, a learned technique, and it comes from a person who has learned to successfully project a "larger than life image" whenever he walks into a room. It begins with the image he has of himself in his own mind, and is complete when his body carries out that image. With practice, anyone can do it. The greatest challenge is consistency, and this is where wearing the proper attire can be of tremendous assistance.

First, establish what that "larger than life image" of yourself will be. Be sure you know clearly what it is (and never tell anyone, it's your secret!). Next, as you dress in your one-step-up attire, imagine that you are putting on that image as you go, like an actor putting on a costume. By the time you finish dressing, you should be completely immersed in your image, and looking back at you in the mirror will be the future you, as you see yourself five or ten years from now.

It's the same principle as when you get dressed for the gym, dressed for golf, dressed for a picnic, or dressed for a night at the opera. The clothes you wear dictate the behavior that should accompany them.

When you are a Presenter, you must embrace that responsibility and behave accordingly, like a leader.

This obscure little technique is your secret to success. Einstein once said, "If you can dream it, you can do it." All you have to do is imagine who you will be in the future, and pretty soon, others will start to see it too, almost in a telepathic sense. They'll begin to see you as the next district manager, the next VP, the next CEO, the next president of the United States.

The key is to develop consistency. If you equate getting dressed in your one-step-up attire with putting on that mantle of authority, then every time you get dressed in that way, you will automatically be putting on that larger-than-life image of a leader. You are well on your way to mastering that elusive yet invaluable element of "presence."

Your Stature

"Each man makes his own stature, builds himself."
—EDWARD YOUNG, *NIGHT THOUGHTS ON LIFE, DEATH AND IMMORTALITY* (1742-1745)

Webster's New World Dictionary defines *stature* as "the height of a person in a natural standing position." In a one-on-one conversation, regardless of someone's actual physical height, or whether they are standing, sitting, or prone, we usually want our fellow conversant to be at our level, so that we can look them in the eye when we are having an exchange. When there is a great height disparity, it is the norm for people to move around, to sit, stand, or kneel, in order to be at about the same eye level as others in the conversation.

It is even the norm to consider people rude when they do not adjust themselves to our height, such as when they stand over us while we are sitting, making us look up at them. Some people take advantage of this and use this knowledge to try to intimidate others. You've no doubt heard the stories about how you can intimidate someone by having a very large, high desk and very low chairs facing it. This is a lame idea, probably promoted by someone with a Napoleon complex.

While it is true that people who use these methods can sometimes succeed in intimidating those unfamiliar with the techniques, they do so on the misguided premise that they can instill the cooperation of the Reactor through the use of fear. This will have a very short-lived and negative effect, and will be interpreted by the Reactor as rude. It is much more effective to use stature to help build an Alliance with your audience than to waste it on intimidation.

Take "One Step Up"

It is the norm, then, to be equal with someone with whom we are having a one-on-one conversation. When it turns into a presentation, however, the situation changes. Suddenly, we want more from the Presenter. We want that Presenter to live up to our concept of a leader, to be someone we can look up to, someone who's "larger than life," worthy of following. By definition, that means someone higher than us or taller than us. Not so high as to intimidate us, yet not so low as to be on the same level or below us. We want someone who is "one step above" us, just like with attire.

Let's face it: On a one-on-one basis, small physical stature is seldom viewed as a plus in a leader. Regardless of how open-minded and unprejudiced we may think we are, we still know that a big guy is generally more powerful than a little guy, thereby offering more protection when we need it (at least, when they are on our side!).

Hollywood understands this concept well. Even in the old days of making Westerns, studios would build their facades small enough to make their short stars look taller, as anyone who's toured the old Universal Studios back lot can confirm. James Cagney stood on many a box to reach the height of his costars.

Even today there are many studies that show there is a much higher percentage of tall people who are CEOs of major corporations than are in the general population. Nor do we see a lot of small people being hired as bouncers, which we consider to be common sense. Obviously, this physical stereotype is the norm, regardless of how distasteful the idea of stereotyping may be.

While it may seem as though your physical stature is beyond your control (short of lifts in your heels), it is, in fact, one of the more adjustable items when making a presentation, providing you are aware of it and know how to adjust for the difference. That's because it isn't stature in itself that makes the difference; it is the Presenter's stature in relation to the Reactor's that makes the difference. Therefore, it is only the appearance of your stature, from the Reactor's point of view, that is ultimately important.

Since a Reactor wants her leader to be someone she can look up to, all you need to do as Presenter is to *create the impression that you are a bit higher, or taller, than your Reactor.* In its simplest form, it could merely mean you stand up to make a presentation rather than remain seated. For example, imagine a staff meeting or a school classroom, where most people are sitting down. When someone sitting down is asked to speak, it is much more effective for that person to stand up to do so. This simple action establishes the authority of the Presenter merely by changing his physical stature to be slightly greater than that of the Reactor.

In addition, standing up allows you to use your full frontal Acknowledgment and eye-contact techniques, which would be impossible from a sitting position.

Standing up will also be interpreted as an act of consideration for the Reactor. When a Presenter stands up, he makes it easier for all of his Reactors to see him. Had he remained seated, chances are fewer Reactors would be able to see him because other seated Reactors would be in the way. It is more difficult to pay attention, or to have a sense of involvement with the conversation, when you can't see the Presenter.

So whenever you are sitting at the same level as everyone else, you must enhance your stature by standing up before speaking. Should you already be standing, and at the same level as everyone else, you must get higher, by standing on a step, a stage, a chair, or a table before you begin to speak.

When there is absolutely no way to raise your stature physically to be higher than your Reactor's, then you must do so psychologically by moving to an area of the room where everyone must turn to look at you. (The center of the longest wall is the easiest place to get the most attention.) Though the latter may not change your physical level, it will, to a limited degree, gain a sense of higher esteem inasmuch as you have taken control of the Reactors by making them all look at you as you stand alone.

Whatever the situation, you must be aware that the Reactor *needs* you to appear to have authority, and is predisposed to give it to someone who appears to have greater stature. As the Presenter, you must satisfy that need by raising your stature "one step up" in whatever way you can in those circumstances.

Stature Behind a Lectern

A real challenge arises when a lectern is involved. Even though the lectern may be raised above your Reactors, it is your relationship to the lectern that now becomes the deciding factor in the impression of stature you make.

Ideally, when you stand behind a lectern, your Reactor should be able to see you *from the waist up*, though from the chest up is also acceptable. This will depend on several factors, such as how far below you your Reactors are, at what angle they will see you in relation to the lectern, the height of the lectern, and so on.

If you are tall, you will seldom have problems with the height of the lectern diminishing your stature. Lecterns are built on the stereotype that leaders are taller than average. Unless you are extraordinarily tall (over about six foot six), you should have no difficulties with a typical lectern. If you are shorter, however, you must overcome several challenges.

Let's begin with the proper placement of the lectern in relationship to you, whatever your height may be. For most Presenters and most sloped lecterns, *the lower edge of the lectern should be about the same height as the waist of the Presenter*.

Fortunately, in some cases, the lectern is adjustable. Larger, more elaborate lecterns often have a hydraulic or electrical adjustment, requiring a simple flick of a toggle switch to move it to the appropriate height for each speaker. Sometimes there is an adjustment that can be made manually through a variety of mechanical means; however, should that be the case, that should be taken care of before the event, which we will discuss in greater detail later. You should always be aware of the capabilities of the lectern under such circumstances, and should make the proper adjustments whenever possible.

When the Presenter is short and the lectern has no high-tech capability to change its height to the correct proportional stature, it may be necessary to employ the low-tech method of a box or platform. Though the appearance of stepping up may seem a bit silly at first, the impression lasts for only a moment, and the Reactor will soon forget what she saw in that instant. The alternative is to stay hidden behind the lectern throughout the entire presentation, a constant reminder of your reduced stature.

One memorable example was back in 1989 when President George H. W. Bush announced the nomination of Senator John Tower for the post of secretary of defense. When six-foot-four President Bush stepped out from behind the lectern, which of course was set for him, and five-foot-two John Tower stepped in to speak, he literally disappeared. He could not be seen behind the lectern and its thicket of microphones. Was it any wonder his nomination never turned into a confirmation? Who would ever believe a person with that small of a stature, who couldn't even overcome the challenge of an overpowering lectern, could be in charge of defending our nation?

Yet the problem could have easily been solved by lowering the lectern or having a box to stand on. Then the Reactor would have seen the same amount of the senator's body above the lectern as she saw of the president's. They would have both appeared to have had the same stature, despite the disparity in their actual height, simply because their relationship to the lectern was the same.

Whether the senator would have eventually been confirmed had he demonstrated the right stature during his opening press conference is debatable, of course, but the fact that he didn't, the fact that he appeared so helpless and his stature so small, was predictably the beginning of the end of his nomination.

Of course, when a lectern is involved with your presentation, there is much more to know than simply how to appropriately adjust your stature when standing behind it. The lectern, and other technical elements used during higher level presentations, are the next tools of the presentational toolbox you must master.

The Lectern

Why stand on the shoulders of titans when we have two
fine feet of clay of our own.
—CLIFTON FADIMAN (1904–1999), EDITOR, AUTHOR, AND RADIO HOST

The first piece of equipment with which most speakers must contend is the lectern (also called a "podium," though that label is technically inaccurate. A podium is actually the platform on which the speaker stands, among other things.). Amazingly, a large number of bad habits that a Presenter acquires stem from the misuse of the simple, ordinary lectern.

The greatest yet most common abuse is when a Presenter leans on the lectern, placing his hands, fingers, forearms, and even elbows on it to support himself. Make no mistake, leaning on a lectern does not make you appear "engaged" as is so commonly promoted. It makes you look tired, lazy, and weak.

This simple act of needing support from a piece of furniture does unimaginable damage to the authority of a Presenter. As Presenter, you must always appear to be in control, beginning with self-control, and that means standing on your own two feet! An Alliance with a lectern grabber is nearly impossible, for who would believe a Presenter could hold up his end of the bargain when he can't even hold up himself without help?

Let's see what happens when you grab hold of a lectern. Immediately, the rigidity of the lectern transfers itself to you. Often you lock your elbows so that you can lean on it. The result is that your arms are stiff, and then they get shoved up into your shoulders. Your scrunched-up shoulders then make you look like a no-neck fullback, a generally less-than-attractive posture.

Worse, it very often makes your clothes (particularly if you're wearing a jacket) bunch up in the back, adding an ugly dose of untidiness. No matter how well thought out your attire, it could all be for naught when you lean on a lectern so hard it scrunches your shoulders into a bunch.

So let's say you've managed to get past locking your elbows, and you're simply holding on to the sides of the lectern. Now try to turn to your first focus. What happens? You are unable to turn your full frontal attention to that focus! From the Reactor's point of view, you will have your arm across your body, and your shoulders will be all askew, making your posture look like that of a hunchback, and the Reactor will know she is not receiving the full attention she deserves.

Even worse, some Presenters won't even try to turn their body, they'll just turn their head. So let's say you've turned your head to one focus. Now turn your head to the other side focus. Now back again, and back again, back and forth. Remind you of anything? Like the silly toy dog in the back of the car window, or an audience watching a tennis game?

Worst of all, sometimes a Presenter will hardly even move his head, he'll just move his eyes back and forth. Back to that horrible and untrustworthy shifty-eyed look again!

When you are glued to the lectern, it prohibits you from using any of the methods previously discussed. You will be unable to turn your body to a full frontal stance, unable to make natural eye contact with your focus, and most important, your ability to gesture will be completely gone—this robs you of one of your most important, valuable, and normal physical elements.

You must realize that the lectern is only to hold your notes and possibly a microphone, and nothing else. Leaning on or laying over the top of a lectern, on your elbows or hands, or anything else, will make it impossible to build the respect and authority you need to create an Alliance. Your mother, teachers, and nuns were all right: Slouching is unattractive. Stand up straight!

The Microphone

That's called a microphone. It's a big sausage that picks up everything you say . . .
—PRINCE CHARLES

In many cases, a presentation will be electronically amplified through the use of a microphone. A microphone is both a curse and a blessing: a blessing because it allows you to use a full range of volume without having to be concerned about reaching the back row, and a curse because Presenters seldom seem to know how to use them effectively. In fact, many times the Presenter's use of the microphone is so inane and awkward as to be comical—certainly not the intended effect.

In the most ideal situation, a microphone should be entirely in the control of a technician, so that you never need be concerned about it at all. A technician should be available to turn the microphone on, test that the volume setting is correct, and set it at the proper height for you prior to the event. Alas, such perfect circumstances seldom exist.

When you as the Presenter are left to handle the microphone on your own, it is essential that you know exactly what must be done with it and why. Since your contact with the microphone usually occurs during those extremely critical first few moments of your appearance, how you handle a microphone can definitively set the tone for your entire presentation.

The first and greatest concern you must have with a microphone, of course, is its correct placement in front of your mouth. Unfortunately, here's what usually happens: When the Presenter first approaches the lectern, he usually employs the easily recognizable "hit-or-miss" principle of microphone placement. This consists of a profoundly unattractive series of actions that generally begin with the Presenter grabbing the microphone, sometimes with two hands, and attempting to wrestle it into place, often into shapes and twists the microphone was never intended to go. Very often, this snake-wrestling exercise is accompanied by an earsplitting whine of feedback (which happens any time you cover up a working microphone) that will have the Reactor cringing and covering her ears before you know it. Not a good start.

Understanding how bad this looks and how helpless some Presenters are in figuring out the correct placement of the microphone, some lectern manufacturers are now building lecterns with microphones on long thin holders that are fixed solidly in place. Any attempt to move them (as they are designed to be immovable) will be in vain. When you do try to move them (as John Kerry kept trying to do during his 2004 presidential campaign, for example), it makes you appear weak and ineffective. After all, if you can't get control over a simple microphone, why should a Reactor let you take authority over her?

Once the Presenter has pushed the mike to a place of his own liking (usually the wrong place), he then asks the ridiculous and highly insulting query, "Can everyone in the back hear me?" (All together now . . . "If we couldn't hear you, how could we hear you ask?") This from someone who want us to join his Alliance!

Obviously, there are only three possible outcomes of microphone placement, which once again follow the Goldilocks principle: too close, too far, and just right.

Too Close

Let's look at what happens in a normal conversation. When someone covers his mouth while speaking (other than during a cough or a sneeze), he inevitably creates the impression that he is saying something secret, or worse, that what he is saying is inappropriate, improper, or insulting, and therefore must be kept away from public consumption. Very often, the Reactor's natural paranoia will rear its ugly head, and she will believe that what is being said behind the Presenter's hand must be bad comments about her or he wouldn't have to hide his mouth.

What's more, hiding one's mouth during a conversation is unnatural. We are used to being able to see the lips of someone talking, and can glean a lot of valuable information from what the lips are doing, whether a Presenter is smiling or frowning, whether the remarks being made are intended to be serious or a joke.

By taking away the Reactor's ability to see his mouth, the Presenter is inadvertently providing another opportunity for her alarm bells to go off. Remember, when alarm bells are ringing, the Reactor can hear little else.

What is most important here is that as Presenter, you must avoid letting the microphone cover any portion of your mouth or face, because it creates the same emotional and negative effect as if you were covering your mouth with your hands.

Unfortunately, many Presenters believe in the "rock 'n' roll" principle of microphone use, placing the microphone as high and as close to their mouth as possible, allowing them to "eat it" like a heavy metal singer. Let's remember one very important thing: The kind of microphones you find on a lectern are designed for the specific purpose of picking up the sound of a voice and electronically projecting it. That means, you, the Presenter, do not need to augment it any further by getting as close to it as possible. (Rock singers *want* to be loud, and have a mixing board to add all kinds of distortions to make them sound better than they are. As a Presenter, you have no such need!)

When a microphone covers a Presenter's face, it is also an indication that the Presenter is being dominated by something apparently out of his control, and again, a Reactor will be reluctant to join an Alliance with a Presenter who is so obviously not in control of his surroundings.

Of course, as Presenter, you must also consider whether your mouth is covered by the microphone from the Reactor's point of view, rather than simply your own. Since Presenters are very often raised above their audience, on a platform, dais, stage, or head table, it is necessary to adjust for those at the lowest angle, or sightline. This means that a microphone must be at least far enough below your face so that even those in the front row will see the microphone *below* your mouth and face.

From a technical standpoint, having the microphone too close to the mouth creates additional problems, most notably when pronouncing any word that contains the letter "p." The force of air necessary to originate the sound of a "p" almost invariably creates a short, staccato popping sound, which, when amplified, will momentarily startle the Reactor.

It will then take a moment for the Reactor to realize what has happened, at which point she will have to classify the information and tuck it away, just as she does with any other image that comes in contact with her. During that moment, she will have lost track of what the Presenter has said in the meantime, and will have to refocus back to the Presenter. This entire distraction can be avoided simply by positioning yourself slightly farther away from the mike, which will reduce the popping sound.

Too Far

On the other hand, of course, having the microphone too far away creates the obvious problem of not being heard at all. When you are not at least close enough to the mike for it to pick up your voice, no one beyond the first row will hear you. You can determine proper distance from the mike by having a partner or a technician check the mike with you prior to the beginning of the event. When you are on your own, you can usually tell you have enough volume when you can hear your own voice gently bounce back at you from the rear wall. (If it hits you in the face, turn it down!)

With some experience, you will soon be able to tell whether the microphone is too far away, or, as sometimes is the case, the sound system is inadequate for the situation. When it is clear that your audience is having trouble hearing you (rest assured, they'll let you know, either by cupping their ears or yelling out, "We can't hear you!") you must compensate by moving the microphone closer than is normally recommended, or raising your own volume should the system be inadequate.

If all else fails, ask your Reactors to please move closer (always a good thing to have them closer anyway), then wait for them to finish moving before starting to speak again. When they know you are waiting for them they will move faster, plus it will insure that every Reactor hears every word, rather then being distracted by all that movement.

Angled Incorrectly

In addition to appropriate distance, the angle of the mike must also be considered. When the head of a microphone points downward, like the curved neck of a swan, or at a straight 90-degree angle to your body, much of your voice will travel over the top of the mike and will miss being amplified completely.

Ideally, a microphone should point upward at about a 60-degree angle, aimed directly toward the second button down on a man's dress shirt or a woman's blouse, and at a distance somewhere between eight to twelve inches from the speaker's mouth. In this way, the voice will project directly toward the head of the microphone, both when the Presenter is looking down toward his script and out toward his Reactors.

All the Right Moves

Properly positioning the mike while you are standing directly in front of the lectern is just the beginning. Now you have to be aware of the position of the microphone in relation to you when you begin changing your focus, lest your body movement take you so far out of position that you create other volume problems.

Very often, when a novice Presenter turns to a side focus, he tends to move *toward* that side focus. Unfortunately, this puts the microphone behind the speaker's mouth. If you have done the full frontal contact exercise we recommended earlier (page 78), then you should already have conquered this challenge. If you skipped it or have forgotten it, now would be a good time to go back and review this important skill.

When you are standing behind a lectern with a microphone, you should realize that when you make a turn, you must *open up* to the side focuses by shifting your weight or slightly stepping *back* rather than forward to the new focus. If you improperly turn by moving forward to address a side focus, rather than slightly to the back, that forward movement may place your mouth nearly in front of or to the side of the head of the microphone, as shown in Figure 8. Your voice would then fall outside the microphone's range.

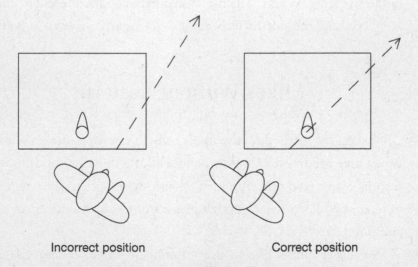

Incorrect position   Correct position

Figure 8. Aligning Your Body with the Microphone

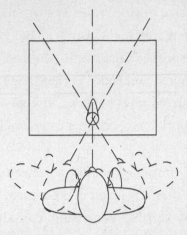

Figure 9. Pendulum Angle of Microphone

Fortunately, a Presenter who is aware of his position as he turns to his new focal point can easily turn to a side focus and keep the microphone in a direct line between his mouth and the new side focus. Imagine a pendulum, with the microphone as the fulcrum and the Presenter as the swinging weight. The direct line between the Presenter, the microphone, and the side focus becomes very clear, as shown in Figure 9.

Mikes Without Lecterns

Obviously, the methods above apply only to microphones on a lectern. When they are freestanding or handheld, the most important consideration is to avoid covering your mouth in the "rock 'n' roll, eat it" style, and to keep it far enough away from your mouth to avoiding popping your "p's."

Some Presenters like to use a handheld mike so they can move around from behind the lectern. This strategy has pros and cons.

Many times when the Presenter comes out from behind a lectern, he tends to wander, seemingly without direction, which detracts from the sense of control and focus he might otherwise project. While there are methods to help overcome the inherent weakness in that style, the biggest problem with using a handheld mike is that the Presenter's gesturing is restricted to just one hand, which limits his ability to capture the norm of a conversation. It is seldom the best strategy.

When using a lavaliere microphone (the kind that are small and clip onto your clothes), the best position for it, again, is about at the second button down on a dress shirt or blouse or its equivalent on whatever you're wearing. Too high and it will essentially be "behind" your mouth, too low and your voice will travel over the top of it.

In any event, whatever type of microphone you are using, be sure to check its projection level prior to your appearance to insure your voice carries to everyone when you are speaking in a conversational tone. Remember to consider the size and ambiance of the room and its decor, as previously discussed.

If used properly, a microphone can provide you with the freedom to adjust your own vocal volume in accordance with the images in your message, rather than any other physical limitations. So naturally, it is best to have some kind of electronic enhancement whenever practical in order to meet the norms of the Reactor. In this way, your use of volume will be the most natural, thereby the most supportive of a one-on-one communications strategy.

The Teleprompter

It has become common practice in many situations for a Presenter to use a teleprompter, a mechanical device that projects the Presenter's script onto one, two, and sometimes even three screens in front of the Presenter, thus eliminating the need to refer to a script on the lectern.

While obviously intended to help the Presenter, teleprompters often create more problems for a Presenter who is unaware how to use them, as there are many pitfalls for the novice. Again, it is simply another presentational tool that can be easily mastered, and by incorporating many of the methods you've already learned here, you can easily eliminate these problems.

The typical setup for a teleprompter for speeches is two screens, one on either side of the lectern, with the Presenter reading alternately between each screen. It should be noted that they are usually placed, quite conveniently, at each of the Presenter's side focal points. When you've mastered the ability to turn to your side focuses for each thought byte in other presentational situations, using teleprompters will be very easy for you.

First of all, let's remember that when you are turning focuses, the right way is to always begin with your feet first, followed by your body, and finally finish the turn by bringing your eyes to the new focus. The first time you use a teleprompter, however, you will have a very strong urge to break that pattern.

That's because you know that your next words are waiting for you on the screen at your new side focal point. As soon as you finish at one side focus, your tendency will be to hurry up and look for your next sentence on the teleprompter at your other side focus. Your eyes will move first, with the rest of your body following. You must resist this urge at all costs!! It is the first thing that goes wrong when someone starts to use a teleprompter.

As mentioned previously, leading with the eyes will make you look shifty-eyed, period. When your eyes move first and your body follows sometime later, it unavoidably disrupts the norms and creates negative effects within the Reactor, as all she will see is that shiftiness in your gaze.

In addition to making sure your feet move first when you are changing focus, you *must* remember not to lean on the lectern. When you lean on the lectern when using teleprompters, it will immediately create the detrimental tennis-watching, head-bobbing repetitiveness that will drive the Reactor crazy.

When Things Go Awry

Be aware that there are many things that can go wrong with teleprompters. The panels can be set at the wrong height or at the wrong angle, which can make the script difficult, sometimes impossible, to read. Teleprompter operators come in all levels of proficiency, so make sure you hire a reputable professional to set up and run the equipment correctly.

Other times, the computer operating the teleprompter could have a complete meltdown, in which case the script is entirely lost. It pays to have a backup hard copy of your script, in your (preferably) leather notebook, with you at all times.

Quite simply, teleprompters are a valuable tool when used in conjunction with the methods you've learned here; however, they can be absolutely destructive when used improperly. By adopting the methods recommended throughout this book, you will find that the teleprompter can be a very effective enhancement to your communication.

PART 5

At the Venue

The Six Final
Insights to Master

Now that all of the preparation before the event has been done, it's time to apply it all in an actual situation. There are countless types of venues in which you might have to make a presentation, yet by understanding the reasons why you should do something in a few sample venues, you should be able to apply it to nearly every venue you might come across. Here we go!

On Site Before the Event

Luck is when preparation meets opportunity.
—ANONYMOUS

As the Presenter, you should try, whenever possible, to arrive at the venue before the audience does, in order to take the opportunity to become familiar with the room. Upon your arrival, you should walk around the room, getting a feel for its size and acoustics as discussed earlier.

You should stand behind the lectern, make sure that it is the right height, and see whether it is adjustable. If someone before you changes that height, you'll want to know how to change it back. If it's not the right height, change it now while you have the chance. If it turns out to be the wrong height for someone else, let him change it. If he didn't bother to learn how, too bad; he should have come in and checked it as you did.

Check out the lighting and sound if possible, both on the lectern and in the room. Check that the reading light on the lectern, if there is one, is functioning properly, and decide whether you're going to need it. If possible, check that any spotlights to be used are properly aligned; this will prevent a direct blinding light or a reflecting glare, which might interfere when you read your script or notes.

You should check the microphone to see if it can be moved (truly, there's nothing worse than watching someone try to move an immovable mike), and to ensure that it points at the correct angle upward toward the second button down on your dress shirt or the equivalent. You should check the sound level by having a helper stand at the back to confirm that you can be heard, taking into consideration that there will more noise when the room is filled with people.

Naturally, you should report any problems immediately to the person coordinating the event, and check them again immediately upon adjustment. Honestly, a good technical staff will appreciate a Presenter who knows what he needs, and will generally do everything possible to accommodate you, as that is their job. Their frustration comes in when the Presenter doesn't know what to ask for, then complains later because something isn't right.

Even when no professional technical staff is present, it is a safe bet that *somebody*, somewhere in the host group, has been given responsibility for providing adequate technical support, and they, too, will welcome the chance to satisfy your needs.

Once you have assured yourself that your technical needs have been met, you should take a moment to select approximately where your focal points will be, and walk the path you will be expected to walk when you are introduced. You should take note of any steps, ledges, wires, or curtains that must be navigated, so that no unexpected trips or falls (a Presenter's worst nightmare) occur during your entrance or approach to the lectern.

Finally, you should spend a few moments behind the lectern, with or without speaking, and get as comfortable with that space as if you were in your own office, behind your own desk. This is your workspace for this event, and it should feel as familiar as possible.

Naturally, all of this preparation can occur only if you arrive early enough to perform these tasks without an audience. We highly recommend that you—particularly if you are a less-experienced Presenter—arrive sufficiently early to carry out this procedure, even when it means you will have time to kill before your presentation. You might even consider doing your walk-through, then leaving and coming back again later for the presentation. There can seldom be too many precautions or too much preparation.

Should an audience already be present by the time you arrive, you will simply have to make these mental observations as best you can prior to the beginning of your presentation, though this leaves much more to chance. Nevertheless, knowing what to look for as you wait to make your presentation can do much to preserve your integrity and confidence.

As the Event Begins

*Nature has given men one tongue, but two ears, that we
may hear from others twice as much as we speak.*
—EPICTETUS

Obviously, what occurs between the time of your arrival to the time
of your presentation will vary depending on the situation. In some
cases, you may be obliged to socialize with your hosts; however, as a
general rule, you should remain isolated from your Reactors for as
long as possible prior to the beginning of the event.

As every professional performer knows, making an entrance can
be a very valuable tool, creating quite desirable anticipation within
the Reactor. Provided this anticipation is used properly (rather than
abused, such as arriving much later than expected), it can prove to be
quite useful in establishing the right kind of authoritative image.

In general, there are two distinct types of public events: those
where the Presenter remains in view prior to his presentation, such as
dinner speeches and panel discussions, and those where the Presenter
remains off-stage or in another room until he has been introduced, at
which time he moves to the lectern and stands alone on the podium.

Since the events that occur *after* arriving at the lectern are the same, let's take a look at what needs to occur before that time.

When the Speaker Remains in View

When you must remain in view of the audience during your introduction or others' presentations, it is extremely important that you give your full attention to every other Presenter who speaks before you. This may sound obvious, yet when you take notice of how poorly many people behave toward a speaker as they sit at a head table, you'll see this is a necessary reminder.

When you pay attention to those who speak before you, it serves several purposes. First, it demonstrates that you are a courteous person—a universally desirable trait, especially in a potential ally to the Reactor. When you fail to pay attention, when you let yourself be distracted by your surroundings, your dinner, your friends in the crowd, or your own notes or script, your movements will pull focus from the current Presenter. Reactors will find themselves looking at you, wondering what you are doing, rather than listening to what that other Presenter is saying.

It is extremely discourteous to appear to ignore other Presenters. It telegraphs to the Reactor that you don't feel the other Presenters are important. When a Reactor sees you ignoring another Presenter, your apparent lack of respect will come across loud and clear. When you set a precedent that it is acceptable to ignore other Presenters, chances are *you* will be ignored when your turn arrives.

When you do pay attention to the current Presenter, you are telegraphing to the Reactor that what that Presenter is saying is important, and should be listened to. When she sees you paying attention, she, too, will pay attention. You have, in fact, put in a Cause to create leadership (you looked), and she follows you by reacting with the Effect (she looks). She is already behaving as your Reactor, and you haven't even said a word!

At the same time, you have also indicated to your Reactor that you are alike, that you are both Reactors at this moment in time, that you are both experiencing the same thing, that you are connected by this mutual event. In other words, you are already accomplishing the first step in your Formula for Inspiration, by identifying with your Reactor, again, without saying a word.

When you are part of a team of Presenters making a unified presentation, this becomes even more important. A Presenter who fails to listen to someone on his *own* team will diminish the authority of himself, the entire team, and the team's message as well.

Finally, by paying close attention to the previous Presenters, becoming a Reactor yourself for that moment in time, you focus your mind on something besides your own upcoming speech. This waiting period can sometimes be a bit destructive, particularly for less experienced Presenters, allowing nerves to pile up and up. Provided you are sufficiently prepared, it is much more constructive to use this time to open the doors toward identifying with your Reactor than to be worried about what will come soon enough.

The Introduction

*The hardest part of a lecture is waking up the audience after
the man who introduces me has concluded his remarks.*
—ANONYMOUS

First and foremost, whenever possible, you should arrange to have someone introduce you. By doing so, you automatically create authority. The Reactor will see that you are important enough to *have* someone introduce you, which has a credibility factor all its own, and will respond with suitable respect for your position.

In addition, you should provide the introduction, or at least the information you wish to be included in the introduction. This will save you from having to say anything about yourself at the beginning of your presentation, which, as you already know, is generally very bad form. You can also tailor the introduction to suit the particular group of Reactors and/or that particular presentation.

Let's see what normally happens during an introduction. While the Introducer is extolling the Presenter's virtues, the Reactor, at some point, will be compelled to turn her attention from that Introducer to you, the Presenter-in-waiting. This is such a strong tendency that even during televised presentations, the camera will almost always get a view of the person being introduced at some point during that introduction.

The impression made at that moment is an incredibly lasting one, so that moment must be everything it can be. Unfortunately, more often than not, that moment is wasted and often sets a bad tone for the rest of the presentation.

For example, should the Reactor find that the Presenter-in-waiting is looking someplace other than toward the Introducer—such as at other people or distractions in the back of the room, at his plate, his fingernails, or his notebook—the Reactor will start to wonder what it is the Presenter *is* looking at. In fact, the Reactor may be so intent to find out what is so fascinating to the Presenter that she will become distracted from what the Introducer is saying about him, and she will hear none of the introduction. If she doesn't hear the introduction, which is designed to demonstrate the Presenter's authority and credibility, then he has lost an opportunity to establish one of the most fundamental necessities of his presentation.

Whenever a Presenter fails to pay attention to the Introducer, the Reactor will likely interpret his inattentiveness as an indication that the introduction lacks importance. When a Presenter decides something isn't important enough to listen to, the Reactor gets that message loud and clear, and responds in kind. After all, if he, her potential leader, doesn't think the information is important enough to pay attention to, why should she? Again, if she doesn't hear the introduction, he's lost ground.

Just as with previous Presenters, you must focus on your Introducer with rapt attention, in order to telegraph to your Reactor that what the Introducer is saying is important. Your attention must be unwavering throughout the entire introduction, with one momentary exception: a quick nod of acknowledgment at the appropriate moment. As mentioned earlier, at some point during the introduction, the audience will be compelled to look at you. When you sense that happening (and you will if you are attuned and waiting for it), it is perfectly acceptable and highly recommended that you briefly turn to your audience and give a short nod of acknowledgment. This will meet the minimum standards of the norm of that situation. Once you have completed the nod, you should immediately return your focus to the Introducer.

This again will telegraph to the Reactor that while you have invited her into the conversation with an acknowledgment, it will also remind her that the Introducer is, for that moment in time, the one requiring our attention. She will quickly follow your look and return her attention to the Introducer.

Obviously, this situation only applies when you are in view of your Reactors prior to your presentation, and particularly during the introduction. When you are coming out from backstage or another room, you need only be concerned with getting to the lectern. Before we discuss that, however, we have to deal with the reality that most Presenters will be feeling at this point: a case of the butterflies.

The Adrenaline Factor

It should be evident that when you have everything we've just discussed to think about and to do while waiting for your presentation to begin, you will have much less time to get nervous about it. The nervousness felt by a Presenter prior to his presentation, however, is both expected and absolutely essential. In fact, it can be one of the more useful tools at your disposal, provided you handle it properly.

It is useless to try to get rid of that nervous energy because frankly, that's nearly impossible for all except the most experienced or hardened Presenters. Rather than ignore it, and risk having that adrenaline overwhelm your good senses, it is better to learn to channel it into something productive.

By recognizing that this rush of adrenaline is inevitable, you will also realize that *where* the adrenaline goes is controlled only by where you choose to send it. Just as we can use it to miraculously flip over cars in a crisis, we can direct it wherever we want it to go, as long as we decide ahead of time where that will be.

The natural tendency is for that adrenaline to go where your body thinks it is needed at the moment it is released, and it will usually first present itself in the movements you make on your way to the lectern.

Very often a Presenter will literally bound out of his chair or from backstage, then race to the lectern as fast as possible, hopefully not tripping over his own feet or other obstacles along the way.

Usually that leap is followed by the Presenter grabbing the lectern to try to stop his forward motion, or to calm himself. Once he grabs hold of the lectern, of course, all of the other destructive, contortionist things already mentioned will start to occur.

Chances are the race to the lectern did little to quell the adrenaline anyway, so the next place it manifests itself is in the speaking mechanism. Out of control, the Presenter usually starts talking as fast as he can. Often that talking begins while he's wrestling the microphone into place, and continues as he pulls out his notes. Mostly it's gibberish until he gets himself set, further confirming his lack of preparation. All the while, he's probably frantically trying to catch eye contact with as many people as possible, which, of course, creates the dreaded shifty-eyed look right off the bat.

Even after the Presenter has his microphone and notes in place, that adrenaline is still likely circulating, looking for somewhere else to be expended. That usually translates into very rapid speaking at the beginning of the presentation, exactly the opposite of what we need at this point. Remember, we want our Reactor to settle into the sound of our voice, so we must speak even more slowly at the beginning than we normally would.

Eventually, after several minutes or more, the Presenter might finally recover from his frenetic moments, his adrenaline will finally settle down, and he might start to make some sense. A great deal of time and energy has been wasted, however, and it will be a struggle for him to gain (or rather, regain) his authority, which has predictably suffered from a weak opening.

Releasing Your Nervous Energy

Our recommendation is simple. As soon as it is time for you to move toward the lectern, *start by taking a deep breath* to quell the surge of adrenaline. Next, visualize that adrenaline as a bubble of energy loose in your body (sort of like the submarine in the old movie *Fantastic Voyage*), heading willy-nilly a\round inside you, potentially causing all this frenetic behavior.

Now, take charge of that bubble. Mentally control the movement of that bubble away from all the potentially disastrous places—in particular, your mouth. As soon as you can visualize it, send that bubble as far away from your mouth as possible: down your legs, down to your feet, and finally, out the bottom of your shoes as you walk toward the lectern.

Whether you are coming from offstage or on the platform, your brain will direct that energy exactly where it has been told: out the bottom of your feet, down to the center of the earth. In your mind, you will be squashing bubbles of adrenaline at each step. By the time you reach the lectern, even if it's only a few steps, you will have significantly reduced your anxiety level, simply because you knew how to get rid of that excess energy.

Should there still be any remaining energy when you arrive, you can release it with an exuberant, "Thank you!" to your Introducer while shaking hands. This should release any final traces of excess energy. Finally, you should complete the movement with another deep, calming breath, if necessary. Chances are, though, that by the time you reach the end of this book, and know what to do every second leading up to and following this point, you will have your energy completely under control, and will not need this final step.

Having released the surge of your pent-up adrenaline through your visualization, you can now moderate any remaining adrenaline evenly throughout your presentation. You should be able to direct any ongoing flow of energy toward more practical things, such as channeling it into enthusiasm, passion, vocal dynamics, long pauses, or whatever else your presentation demands.

Every Presenter is well advised to consider a visual path with which to distribute that excess adrenaline. Whether you decide to squash adrenaline bubbles under your feet or select some other mental image, you should be mentally prepared to send your adrenaline someplace far away from you as soon as possible.

Now that you have fully considered your adrenaline and determined how to deal with your excess energy, let's take a look at the final moments before your presentation, and how to make the absolute most of them.

The Looking/Listening Ratio

All speech, written or spoken, is a dead language, until
it finds a willing and prepared hearer.
—ROBERT LOUIS STEVENSON

As we've noted before, it is difficult to both look at and listen to something at the same time. Your brain must make the choice to let one or the other dominate because it can only create and file one image at a time. Because most presentations, by their nature, predominantly involve listening, your goal as a Presenter, obviously, is to encourage your Reactor to be listening as much as possible.

Vision, however, is one of the most advanced senses we humans have. Whenever something new comes to our attention, our first instinct is to visually inspect it very carefully. This obviously developed as a means of survival, allowing us to analyze what we see until we can understand and catalog it, to determine whether what we see will harm us or feed us. Only when our visual inspection is nearly complete do our other senses become involved.

The same is true for Reactors to a presentation. When your Reactor first turns her attention to you, about 80 percent or more of her initial inspection is done by *looking*. She will analyze what she sees until she can understand and catalog this new image satisfactorily. She will proceed to judge how alike or different you are from her, whether you meet the norms of what she was expecting, whether you are a friend or a foe.

This is the moment when all of the valuable preparation you have made will come into play. You must now let your Reactor thoroughly "check you out." Since you have put in the Causes to get the Effect of your Reactor's approval, through your attire and personal image, then your success is predictable, even inevitable. This throws the door wide open for the conversation that is to follow, and the possibility that, in the end, an Alliance will be formed. This moment can begin at several different junctures, depending on the particular venue.

Making an Entrance

When you are entering from offstage or from another room, the Reactor begins assessing you the moment you break the curtain or otherwise present yourself in her line of sight. At that instant, every Reactor will be looking at you, making judgments of your leadership qualities based on what you do in the next few moments. You must present yourself in the way that Reactor expects in accordance with the norms of authority, or she will be disappointed.

First and foremost, we expect a leader coming from offstage to make his way to the lectern in a deliberate and forthright manner, with a walk full of purpose and intent, and a businesslike, no-nonsense demeanor. A strong walk will let the Reactor know her time isn't being wasted, as this Presenter is a real leader. Not surprisingly, this kind of walk will come naturally when you are using the suggestion of venting excess energy through the bottom of your feet. It will also insure your posture is straight, another expectation of leadership.

When You're Already Visible to the Audience

Naturally, when you are visible prior to your presentation, at a head table or other position where your Reactor can see you, you must always be aware that your behavior will make an impression with that Reactor. Whether you are eating your meal, speaking with a seating companion, or simply going about the usual niceties, you must be prepared for the ongoing scrutiny. When you put on your image of authority as you put on your clothes, as suggested earlier, you will already be prepared for this. Simply behave in the way we all know a leader should behave.

Be aware, however, that no matter how much your Reactor views you casually prior to your presentation, she will not be able to complete her analysis of you as a leader until after you reach the lectern and she's had a chance to give you a complete visual once-over.

She must overcome one challenge in order to do that, however. Even though our natural instincts are to analyze everything we see to ensure it poses no danger, as we've become more civilized, we have taught ourselves that it is impolite to stare at someone. We grow up being careful to never look directly at a stranger. We might take a peek or even a good long look when there is no chance of getting caught, but we know it is terribly bad form to get caught staring at anyone. When we do get caught, we invariably quickly avert our eyes, even when we believe they want us to look at them, like during the first moments of adolescent flirting.

As Presenter, you need to recognize that your Reactor is compelled by instinct to look at you, but might be afraid of getting caught, because that's a cultural no-no. Even when you are in plain view, she will be loathe to cast all but the most casual glances your way for that reason. She'll want to look, she just won't be able to very effectively. Therefore, you must provide her the opportunity to look at you without fear of getting caught.

You have already provided some of that opportunity by paying close attention to the other Presenters before you. As the other Presenters speak, your Reactor will see that you are so focused on the current speaker that you will not notice her as she peeks at you for a moment or two. This allows her to begin to take her measure of you. She will then quickly return to looking at the other Presenter, as well, because you are indicating in your body language that that is what she should be doing. As we previously mentioned, you have put in the Cause to get the Effect of getting her to look back to the current Presenter, thus making her an instant follower of yours.

This takes us up to the time of your introduction. Again, you are paying full attention to your Introducer, and so is your Reactor. At one point during the introduction it will be appropriate for you to turn and nod to your Reactor, but then you must return your full attention to the Introducer.

Now the moment has come. Your introduction is complete and it is time for you to move toward the lectern. When rising from a seated position, whether you are at the head table or somewhere nearby, you should stand, move behind your seat, and push your seat back under the table. This demonstrates to the Reactor that you are deliberate, organized, and even tidy, strengthening that sense of authority by exhibiting qualities most Reactors will admire in a leader.

Usually when seated, a man or woman wearing a jacket will have it unbuttoned for comfort. Now that you are standing, you should button your jacket. This will put you in a one-step-up position in attire, as everyone still seated has his or her jacket unbuttoned. The buttoning action will probably be blocked from view by the chair, providing you stay there until the task is accomplished.

Once your jacket is buttoned, or you have otherwise straightened out your attire as needed, you should pick up your notebook and *take a deep, calming breath*. This will create a very useful pause, which will accomplish several very positive things. First, it gives you time to visualize your adrenaline bubble and start it on its path to your feet, and to get your feet in the right place before moving forward, a precaution against a possibly embarrassing trip or stumble. Most stumbles occur on the first step or two, due to the Presenter being in an unbalanced position because he tries to move too quickly, usually because of the excess energy.

The deep breath, of course, will also assist in grounding any butterflies you may be experiencing, and buys you another moment to stand up straight and further collect yourself.

Now, you must begin to walk slowly and deliberately to the lectern, looking only at the person who has introduced you, or at the lectern should there be no other person on stage. This is the beginning of letting your Reactor have the opportunity to begin fully "checking you out," so you should never look at the audience as you make your way to the lectern!

Should you look at your Reactor while you are walking to the lectern, you rob her of the opportunity to satisfy that initial visual curiosity, as she will still be afraid of getting caught if you should catch her eye. Therefore, *you should never look toward your Reactor until she has had sufficient time to fully satisfy that curiosity*. This will take only a few moments once the attention has been called to you. Failure to allow her that time now will force her to take that look later—and that will distract her from listening.

Letting the Audience "Check You Out"

During these initial moments, about 80 percent of your Reactor's attention is on looking, and the other 20 percent is on listening, since the only thing to listen to at this moment is the applause after your introduction. If the situation doesn't warrant applause, all the better, because now the Reactor can devote 100 percent of her attention to looking, which will get the visual analysis over with even more quickly.

So the pause that you created by replacing your chair under the table, buttoning your jacket, and deliberating walking to the lectern is extremely valuable. It allows your Reactor time to make the requisite visual catalog and begin to anticipate your first words, and it gives you time to get completely focused. By the time you arrive at the lectern, your Reactor will be waiting, breath bated, for you to begin.

Yet those few steps to the lectern are still not enough time for a complete visual analysis. Even if you spend a moment thanking the Introducer, your Reactor will not have enough time to concentrate on you alone. We know that it would be pointless to try to speak immediately upon arriving at the lectern, because the Reactor is still consumed with looking, and any words would be lost.

Once you arrive at the lectern, place your notebook on it and open to the appropriate pages. Then you must quickly determine whether the microphone is in the correct position, as discussed earlier. When it is, leave it alone! It serves no purpose to unnecessarily monkey around with it.

When the microphone is in the wrong place, take a brief moment to become the technician. Adjust it quickly and efficiently. *Do this without looking at your Reactor*, because the technician should be invisible, and only the Presenter should make eye contact with the Reactor (at the right moment, which is yet to come).

Once the adjustment is complete, take a small step back from the lectern, take a breath, mentally shed the technician role, and reassume the role of Presenter. Finally, look up to your center focus, make firm eye contact, then step forward into the lectern and speak your first words, which should be a simple greeting of, "Good morning/afternoon/ evening." Then begin your first identifying thought byte to your center focus, and continue on from there as previously discussed.

Though it is always better for you to be solely a Presenter and not be forced into the role of temporary technician, you can actually make performing this little task work to your advantage when necessary. Your willingness to take on the role of the technician when needed indicates you are a "hands-on" kind of person who understands what job must be done, and are willing to roll up your sleeves and do what is necessary. Of course, it must be done quickly and efficiently to create the impression that you know what you are doing. Too much time or the appearance of inefficiency, such as the snake-wrestling image, will work to the opposite effect.

It is equally essential, however, that a clear distinction be made when the technician's job is done and the Presenter's job begins, again, to ensure that you demonstrate the appropriate level of authority for the role.

When you are forced to take on the role of technician, such as adjusting the microphone or lectern height, you should never look out into the audience until after you have completed those tasks. Looking into the audience any time before you step up into the lectern will rob them of the opportunity to satisfy their visual need to look at you. The first time you ever look at your Reactor should be as you step into the lectern after having completed your preparatory tasks.

The ease in which this transition takes place will register well with the Reactor, indicating that you are someone who is in enormous control, someone who can be trusted to get the right job done at the right time—just the kind of person with whom a Reactor would like to establish an Alliance. Yet another battle is won before you even open your mouth.

Yes, all of these activities will take time. It will seem like an eternity to you the first time you try this. You'll be convinced that the audience is getting restless because you are taking too long. You'll be overwhelmed with the urge to hurry up. *Resist it.* You must trust in the reality of human nature, that the time spent here is being used wisely and to the benefit of both you and your Reactor.

Finessing the Looking/Listening Ratio

The purpose here is to do everything you can to encourage your Reactor to get as much of her looking out of the way as early and as quickly as possible. You want your Reactor to make the shift from giving 80 percent of her attention to what she *sees* to giving that 80 percent to what she *hears*. You want that shift to occur in time for her to hear your first words, rather than joining you several minutes later. That shift from looking to listening is essential for the conversation to progress.

In ideal circumstances, a Presenter should strive to achieve and sustain a looking/listening ratio of approximately 80 percent listening and 20 percent looking throughout the presentation. When your opening statement is a strong and vivid identifier, followed by a nice long pause, every ear in the room will turn toward you, and the looking analysis will be over. The pendulum will swing toward listening like a compass heading for the North Pole: immediately and directly. This is what needs to be considered with the looking/listening ratio. Once you have her aural attention, you can take your Reactor wherever you want to go, satisfying every need both you and she have.

When Murphy's Law Prevails

Everything that can go wrong will.
—MURPHY'S LAW

You now know exactly what to do to prepare for your presentation, from the content of your message to the layout of your notes or script. You know how to use focuses, even when the room is too large to make eye contact, by using surrogates. You know what you must do with your body language, your voice, and your attire, and how to make the most of the technical tools you have at your disposal. You know that you must simply have a conversation with one person at a time, with a lot of other people eavesdropping.

You are fully prepared to deal with all of the things that normally happen during a presentation, and you should feel more comfortable than you ever thought possible under such circumstances. You are in complete control of everything with which you can be in control. But what happens when something unexpected and out of your control goes wrong?

Of course, there will always be the chance that certain uncontrollable events may occur during your presentation. Regardless of what happens, how you handle these momentary crises will make the most lasting impression of your presentation. When you play your cards right, however, you can also make the most positive impression possible. So when Murphy's Law does prevail, it is essential for you to know how to handle the proverbial worst-case scenario in order to come out smelling like a rose.

In the event of almost any technical malfunction, such as when the microphone stops working, the lights go out, or some other audio or visual difficulty occurs, it is essential you appear to remain *in control*. Maintaining authority is the most effective way to ensure that the level of respect for you remains as high as possible.

Everyone, both Presenter and Reactor, accepts the reality that occasionally, technical difficulties will occur. When they do, there are only three possible outcomes: (1) the Presenter will take complete control of the situation, (2) the Presenter will completely lose control of the situation, or (3) the Presenter merely abdicates control of the situation. The only desirable outcome is the first. Unfortunately, the most natural reaction usually results in one of the last two.

Face the Facts

The most common old wives' tale guiding the Presenter's reaction to technical difficulties is to continue on as though nothing has happened. While this may be expected during a performance of a die-hard theatrical group (which is working in a make-believe world anyway, so the situation can be anything they want it to be, including dark and silent), it is entirely unsuitable for a speaking engagement.

Let's face it: When a Presenter continues unabated through obvious technical problems such as a blackout, he will appear to be utterly disconnected with reality. Such a disconnect will make him look like an idiot. When a Reactor sees a Presenter ignoring the obvious, what in the world is she supposed to expect from him in an Alliance?

Stay in Control

Just as detrimental is when the Presenter stops and points out whatever it is that has gone wrong ("Gee, the lights went out!") as though someone needed to be told! This is usually followed by a request or demand that something be done immediately. When a Presenter has to ask for help, it diminishes his authority, which makes him appear out of control.

Worst of all, the Presenter will try to do something to fix the situation himself. This is a disastrous move, since it means that the Presenter must drop his role of authority and reclaim the role of technician. Since the chances are that he will be unable to fix the problem, he will have demonstrated that he couldn't live up to that lesser role, leaving huge doubt that he is able to live up to his greater role. When a *real* technician comes along to fix it, the humiliation will be complete. No chance of a meaningful connection with the audience after that!

In every case, the Presenter and his message are completely undermined by things that are obviously out of his control. He has been unable to demonstrate his ability to take control, therefore his ability to lead is understandably called into question.

Make Lemonade

Of course, that leaves just one easy and very deliberate way to overcome technical difficulties while maintaining absolute control: Do nothing. As Presenter, you should stop everything you are doing. You should say nothing, except possibly, to your Reactor, a simple, "One moment please." You should then gaze meaningfully, though never angrily or accusingly or frantically, at whoever is in charge of the technical aspects of the event, or the host, should the technical person be out of sight. Then wait.

It should come as little surprise that such a technician, who will suddenly feel an enormous amount of pressure for obvious reasons, will move extremely quickly to the source of the problem. No doubt the technician (or whoever is serving in that capacity) will very hurriedly issue a status report, and will give an estimate of how soon the problem will be resolved.

Without saying a word of explanation, without blaming anyone, without becoming a technician yourself, without having to make any apology, and without skipping a beat, you have succeeded in maintaining every element of control. So much action was accomplished on your behalf, without you having to say a word, that the Reactor is compelled to see you as a person who really gets things done. This is exactly the kind of person with whom she will want to have an Alliance, someone she can trust to get the job done, quickly, effectively, and with panache.

Once the problem is resolved, you need only say, "Thank you for your patience," and begin where you left off, or perhaps repeat the last thought byte prior to the mishap to enforce the last image the Reactor received from you.

You should never try to explain the problem, lest the images you create supersede and distract the Reactor from those already created from your message. Better to let your earlier images sink in further during this extra-long pause, rather than try to replace them with unimportant nonsense that fails to progress the plot.

You should also never try to place blame, nor do anything more than thank your Reactor for her patience. As we mentioned, we all recognize that these things happen, and it only makes sense to be understanding and realistic about it, and carry on as before as soon as possible.

There are few opportunities that hold so much potential danger yet can add such enormous strength to a Presenter's presentation when handled effectively. Once you demonstrate you can successfully overcome such an occurrence without batting an eye, it becomes very apparent to the Reactor that you could likely overcome anything. By virtue of a technical accident, you have made huge strides toward demonstrating that you are just the kind of person she can trust with her future. Your success as a Presenter and a leader are secured.

A Final Note

Speech is power; speech is to persuade, to convert, to
compel. It is to bring another out of his bad sense into your
good sense.
—RALPH WALDO EMERSON

The skills necessary to make an inspirational presentation, whether it be
to one person or millions, can be learned by anyone with enough desire
and discipline. Like every other skill, whether a vocation or a hobby, it
takes practice. Whether you are a novice merely trying to overcome your
fear of speaking in front of a group, an accomplished speaker wishing to
take your art to the highest level, or someone who simply wants to make
the most of your ability, the steps, elements, tools, and insights in the previous chapters will help you reach your goal.

The most important thing to remember is that every communication should result in an Alliance that satisfies both your needs *and* the
needs of your Reactor. Whatever your reasons for making a presentation, by being a dynamic, effective, confident, and inspirational
speaker, you have the opportunity to help countless people lead hap-
pier, healthier, more profitable lives. And that will make the whole
world a better place! Enjoy!

Index

About the Authors

For more than two decades, the Henderson partnership has kept the couple together nearly every moment of every day, enjoying a twenty-four/seven relationship, which both say is "never boring"!

Roy Henderson has more than fifty years of experience in the art of presentation and the study of audience psychology, beginning with baccalaureate degrees in drama, psychology, and acting from the University of London and the Central School of Speech and Drama. As an actor, director, and alumnus of the prestigious Royal Shakespeare Company, he has created, directed, performed, and advised presentations of all kinds on five continents. His proudest acting performance was in the title role of *Henry VIII* for Queen Elizabeth II and the Royal Family during her Silver Jubilee Celebration.

Jeanette Henderson's presentational career began at the ripe old age of seven, and has been augmented by another forty-plus years of communications education and experience. She has been the writer, producer, stage manager, and performer of countless radio, television, and theatrical productions. She is a published author, a political commentator, and a speechwriter, and she is the special correspondent for "Viewpoints," a public radio talk program in Tennessee.

Since 1988, the Hendersons have devoted much of their time to coaching industrialists, community leaders, attorneys, physicians, politicians, and graduate actors in the improvement of their applicable presentation skills. They have shared their presentational skills with the Burt Reynolds Institute for Theatre Training, University of Northern Arizona, Universal Productions, Procter & Gamble, National Pharmaceutical Council, Fleishman Hilliard Public Relations, and scores of others. Roy and Jeanette have served as the official speech coaches and presentation advisors for *every* Republican National Convention since 1992, and have consulted for countless political campaigns.

While they have a home on an isolated mountaintop in Tennessee, they spend much of their time traveling for their company, Podium Master, which provides speech coaching, consultation, and training in the presentational arts to clients of all kinds. They also hold Podium Master retreats at a nearby mountain lodge in historic Beersheba Springs, Tennessee.

Feel free to contact them with your comments on *There's No Such Thing as Public Speaking* through their website, www.theresnosuchthing aspublicspeaking.com. To find out more about Podium Master, visit www.podiummaster.com.

IDEA

pattern of neurons that makes idea
is recreated in the minds of the audience

ideas are capable of changing how people think
shaping how they interact w/ the world

1. Link everything back to single idea
2. Give audience a reason to care
   → make them curious
   → ~~And~~ make a disconnection in their
      worldview that you can gap

3. Build your idea
   — use metaphors
   — ~~test~~ talk on friends

4. Make your idea worth sharing
   → who does it benefit?

* to alleviate nerves
— don't think about yourself
— think about audience